I0434589

The person on the cover depicts both the frustration of walking in bitterness and the way we try to cover up our bitterness when around other people. We may "mask" our feeling for a while, but you can be sure your true feelings will break through the false mask we so often wear in public. It is not God's plan for man to walk in such disorder and fake perception before others. When we allow God to deal with our bitterness and set us free, then we can put the happy, but false mask down and permit others to see the real us! Then we can live in peace with ourselves, others and God.

By: Marvin L. Ward

LuLu.Inc

Ministries of Forgiveness Moto
TO WALK IN FORGIVENESS YOU MUST WALK IN FORGIVENESS

Other Books: The Grace of Justice

Faith Child of Promise

In this book, we will look at two levels of bitterness. Part one will be on the avoidable bitterness and the second part will be on the un-avoidable bitterness. Most people I know actually experience the first part or avoidable bitterness and not the un-avoidable bitterness. However, many in today's society do experience the second part or un-avoidable bitterness. However, both need to come to the same peace only found in forgiveness.

To Walk In Forgiveness You Must Walk In Forgiveness

Avoidable Bitterness

Part One:

Email: <u>iforgive@toforgive.org</u>
Web: www.iforgivetoforgive.org

FORWARD

I have spent many a year, and shed many a tear over bitterness in my lifetime, including experiencing the condemnation it brings. I grew up feeling very rejected in life. As a result, I developed a very low self-esteem of life. My biggest argument when challenged, was always, "But I know how I feel", when someone would try to offer me counsel. Our personal feelings are very real, but very false! I had to learn the truth of God's word of who I really am.

Please read this book and allow the Holy Spirit to guide you to your freedom in Christ from the emotions you fight with every day.

The second part deals with the bitterness we could not have avoided in live but deals with the fact that we need to deal with this bitterness in the company of forgiveness just the same as the first bitterness discusses.

All scripture quoted is from the New King James Version unless otherwise stated.

I wish to dedicate this book to everyone who is troubled with bitterness in their life. I know the pain bitterness can be in life. Thanks to the loving patience of the Holy Spirit in teaching me how to overcome bitterness, I now live a much happier life. I pray that this book will help you as much as it has helped me.

Consider this!

Should you find yourself the victim of other people's bitterness, ignorance, smallness or insecurities; Remember, things could be worse.

You could be one of <u>them</u>!

AVOIDABLE BITTERNESS

UNDERSTANDINGS ABOUT THE BIBLE

Let us begin with a couple of agreements between us!

Some people believe the Bible only contains the Word of God while others believe the Bible is the Word of God! In other words to believe that the Bible only contains part of the Word of God which makes the Bible a little less than God's Holy Word. It now becomes their task to figure out which part is the Word of God and which part are just words of man. One of the main problems with this position is that the part you choose to be the Word of God may or may not be the same part I might choose.

I personally take the stand that the Bible is from beginning to end, from Genesis to Revelation, indeed the Word of God. To believe that the Bible only contains the Word of God, I find that it makes us in disagreement with each other! We will by nature be choosing that part of the Bible pleasing to our mind or that part we can agree with, without contradicting our personal belief and rejecting the part that contradict what I choose to believe! I often find the Word of God is in sharp contrast with my carnal thinking and my carnal thinking does not want to renew the thinking of my mind!

I choose to take the stand with all who believe that the Bible, in its complete form, is the Word of God! This means I believe that the Bible, from cover to cover, is the complete and absolute Word of God. I also believe that the Bible is inerrant in its content. If one believes there is an error in the Word, then it is obvious that the Bible or that subject has **not** been studied sufficiently. The Bible will interpret itself, and reveal the correct meaning once we are willing to search the full truth. Most inconsistencies, which have been shown to me, are shown to me by people who do not believe that the whole Bible is indeed the Word of God and as such render only partial interpretations or inaccurate interpretations! Many will make a misinterpretation of one verse and claim a contradiction! When correct interpretation is applied to both verses, all contradictions will disappear. There is no choosing what is from God. It all is from God. I personally take the position that the Bible is absolutely the complete Word of God.!

Beliefs or 'What I believe is' vs. the Word of God

Please do not come to me with "What I believe is" and expect me to discuss any topic or teaching of the Bible with you! I have learned that the "What I believe is" theology is not based on the Word, but rather is based on what others you have heard have had to say about their ideas. You see it comes from others: a little bit from your mother, grandmother, preachers on radio, preachers at funerals, people speaking on television and who knows who else you have heard speak about God and the Bible, you have set your "ideas" of God on man's ideas rather than the Word of God. Everyone who comes to me with that philosophy I have found always base their belief's on logic and tradition coupled with words they have heard from someone, with a little mixture of the Word to make it sound good. The "What I believe is" theology is always based on second hand information. I consider this type of theology as "Trash Theology" and quite worthless! Quite often, they will try to quote a statement and swear it is from the Bible. Such as, "God helps them who help themselves". I refuse to lower the Word of God to that level of discussion! However, if you come to me with Book, Chapter and Verse, now we have a foundation with which to discuss yours and my belief about what God has to say concerning our relationship or love with each other! When we talk about the

Love of God, I am meaning the Love of God according to the Word, not according to carnal logic or philosophy! I am personally convinced that a person **cannot** have a conviction until they can know the Book, Chapter and Verse of the Bible on the said subject! Any other concept is merely someone's ideas.

Many hold to their traditions as the foundation and final authority of belief. I only believe in traditional teachings that are confirmed in the Word of God!

WHAT DOES LOVE HAVE TO DO WITH IT?

Love has much to do with all our actions. As Carnal man we don't truly understand the concept of loving the loveless. Yet we continually read in the Word about the command of Love. Let us note some of what the commandments are that the Word gives to us.

We are to keep His commandments because we *LOVE* Jesus – In John 14:15 we read, *"If you Love me Keep my commandments"*. To me, that is very simple! Where there is a true love for Jesus from a personal experience with Him as Lord, there is a true desire to submit to the commandments of our Lord. We must decide if Jesus is the love of our life or is this world the love of our life. Jesus declared that

Love a commandment. We read in John 13:34, *"A new Commandment I give to you, that you love one another; as I have loved you, that you also love one another"* Note the last phrase, *"that you also love one another"*, that is me . . . me loving you and you loving me. Note in this passage that I am to love you, not if you deserve to be loved or that if you are loveable, or even if I want to love you, but I am to love you because Christ loved me! That expression of love for one another is the confirmation of our Love for Jesus. I John 2:3, 4 says *"Now by this we know that we know Him, if we keep His commandments. (4) He who says, "I know Him," and does not keep his commandments, is a liar, and the truth is not in him."* Just how plain can God get? How do I know that I love Jesus? The answer is by the way I keep his commandments. To claim that we love Jesus and do not live by his commandments proves us to be a liar. We are like rain clouds without rain.

One of the most prevalent testimonies of not keeping his commandments is demonstrated in not faithfully attending the Church Jesus died for. I find it most amazing that Jesus loved the church enough to die for it, yet we cannot love the church enough to attend. In I John 2:19 John writes *"They went out from us, but they were not of us; for if they had been of us, they would have continued with us; but they went <u>out</u> that they might be made manifest (to render* *apparent), that none of them are of us".* The truth cannot stand out from our lives if it is not there! The Word of God says that our absence is <u>evidence</u> of our public testimony of not being part of the Kingdom of Christ. We can maintain all we want that we are Christians, but if we are able (yet we can attend all the world events or functions) but don't attend church, the Word of God declares that we are in fact **NOT** part of the church. The Word teaches in Hebrews 10:25, that we are **NOT** (under any circumstance) to forsake the assembling of ourselves together. What many do not understand is that to claim to love Jesus and then state that we do not attend church because there are hypocrites there; we have become Satan's greatest witness! We have allowed the enemy to pervert our righteousness into becoming self-righteousness, in that we are now too good to attend church with the hypocrites! Read Luke 18:9-14 again. The Word teaches that Jesus **LOVED** the church so much that He died for it. I ask you, were there hypocrites then? Yet Jesus still died for the church, and we in our *self-righteousness* refuse to attend the same church Jesus died for! Satan loves this kind of testimony! Personally, I prefer to attend with the hypocrites and let the love of Christ in me shine before them! I want them to see the righteousness of Christ in me as opposed to the self-righteousness to which they give testimony.

In I John 1:6 we find these words... *"If we claim to have fellowship with him YET walk in the darkness, we lie and do not live by the truth."* Anyone can say publicly that they walk with Jesus and are a Christian, but if our lives are actually walking in the darkness or absence of love, which includes the love of the Church Jesus died for, we are without a doubt, liars and proves that we do not live by the words we speak. In I John 2:9 we find *"Anyone who claims to be in the light but hates his brother is still in the darkness."* Amazing, but the Word of God declares that to hate or despise a brother or sister for anything means my heart is still walking in the darkness of sin! We simply cannot walk in the light of Jesus and exercise hatred for anyone! You say, but what if..."Well, if I hate Osama Bin Laden", (the al-Qaeda-affiliated leader believed responsible for the destruction of the **twin towers** of the World Trade Center in March 2001), then I am in sin. I heard someone say once that we should pray for the death of a man named Osama Bin Laden; this is walking in darkness and not in the light of Jesus. We do not have the right to hate even Osama Bin Laden, We are allowed to hate the actions he takes toward others and us but we must exercise an attitude of Christian Love toward him if we wish to walk in the light of Jesus. For we find in I John 4:20-21 *"If someone says, 'I love God,' and hates his brother, he is a liar..."* Do you not understand that hate and love together equal a lie? We cannot express our love of God and hatred for another and be true to God! God declares that He will look upon us as liars.

Note verse 21 where God declares that he commands our love to others… *"And this commandment we have from Him; that he who loves God <u>MUST</u> love his brother also."*

Take note of this Scripture – Mark 11:25-26 *"And whenever you stand praying, "If you have anything against anyone, forgive him, that your Father in heaven may also forgive you your trespasses. (26) "But if you do NOT forgive, neither will your Father in heaven forgive your trespasses."*

God equates not liking or no love as bitterness and hate! You do not have the right to declare "but you don't know what he did or said!" You are now judging moral sin as spiritual sin and have lowered yourself to the carnal realm of life. Jesus declares that if you wish to walk in the forgiveness of God you **WILL** forgive your brother and do it **NOW**! I am talking about forgiving the person not the sin committed. You have no right to ask for the forgiveness of God in your personal life if you are not forgiving your brother! This is more serious than murder, rape or any other sin, only of this one sin does God state that if I do not forgive I will not be forgiven! I personally like walking in the forgiveness of my Heavenly Father; therefore, I work at making sure that I am forgiving my brother of what ever I feel he has done to me. Note I am not forgiving the thing I believe he has done, but forgiving my brother personally!

What makes unforgiveness such a serious sin to God? God considers unforgiveness as a direct rebuke to His Love! The word rebuke in the Bible means to consider one's self more correct and seeks to censor the working of God, as in Mat 16:22 *"Then Peter took him, and began to rebuke (to admonish, forbid as to censure) him, saying, Be it far from thee, Lord: this shall not be unto thee."* When a concept is not in agreement with our thoughts, we will 'rebuke' the idea as wrong, believing we know the more correct truth. Forgiving is not good carnal thinking! However, it is very good Biblical thinking! When we think in our mind that we cannot forgive someone, then we 'rebuke' the teaching of forgiveness as not logical, because it is not logical, but very Biblical. Nevertheless, God still insists that we forgive the individual, even though it does not agree with our carnal reasoning. We will never find peace within until we obey the commandment of God to forgive! We do not have the authority to rebuke the love of God! Only when we surrender to the love of God will we learn to forgive and release everything to our wonderful Father.

In Hebrews 12:15-19 we find these interesting words... *"Looking diligently lest anyone fall short of the Grace of God; lest* any *root of bitterness springing up cause trouble, and by this many become defiled;"* How many times have we fallen short of the Grace of God by simply not exercising forgiveness toward someone. Note that just the very root of bitterness will cause trouble and those I love the most will be defiled. God knows we will at times get angry with our brother, but the key is just how long are we allowed to be angry? Note the words of Paul in Ephesians 4:6 *"Be angry and do not sin: do not let the sun go down on your wrath".* If I allow my anger to pass sundown, it becomes bitterness. When I wake up the next morning, I am now in bitterness, which God hates! Each day that bitterness grows a little bigger and soon begins to create trouble in our lives. The ultimate danger is that in time that bitterness will actually begin to affect those around me, especially the ones I actually love. They will soon begin to perceive the bitterness toward another as bitterness toward them. It will actually begin to defile the people I love the most.

When we allow bitterness to become part of our life while claiming to be Christians, we actually become **"Cartoon Christians"**. You have watched cartoons and know that cartoon characters can do anything, they do not have to follow the rules of life! They do not have to follow reason or logic. As "Cartoon Christians", we begin to think we can do as we desire in life and still walk in the love of God.

To hate or to be bitter at someone makes us at war with God! I am no longer walking along side with God but against God. We need to understand that I now hate someone that God loves. I am at enmity with God! I.e....I have declared a greater judgment than that of God, in that I believe I have the right to override the Love of God and hate my brother. After all, since we are down here among our brothers, we think we have a greater view or understand of the need to hate! However, being cartoon Christians we feel we can do both....we can pretend to Love and Hate at the same time! We begin to feel we can walk in darkness and light at the same time declaring that we see the real sin. We are now walking in Satan's theology of 'justified unforgiveness'! Because it is me that is offended, I feel that somehow I am now justified in not forgiving that individual and nevertheless still maintain my love for Almighty God!

We must learn to see others as God see them. This is a little more difficult than just hating those we see doing things against us. We need to ask ourselves these two questions. "Have I never done anything wrong toward God?" and "Was it not my sin that put Jesus on the Cross?", in that I forgotten how deprived and covered with sin my life was before Christ washed me clean with his precious blood? I was once as sinful as the brother I now hate and yet Jesus forgave me! I once was at enmity with God but the blood of Jesus made atonement for me. I thought I could love God and hate my brother also. However, I learned that that was not what the Word taught. To be "at one" with God I **MUST** love the ones God loves. The key is that I <u>must still</u> hate their sin. We must learn to separate them from their sin. To walk in the Spirit we must love our brother while hating his sin. Yes, even the one who said that awful statement or did that terrible deed towards you, you must learn to love. We will learn what to do about their sin later.

IN THIS BOOK I DIVIDE BITTERNESS INTO TWO CATEGORIES.

Avoidable Bitterness: The first session:

We learned in the Word that a right position in Christ would have avoided most of those offenses or anger we often harbor. We need to learn to show that God is correct, and not our feelings! We must learn how to deal with offenses even when we "feel" we are 100% right!

Unavoidable Bitterness: – The second session:

A lesson taught in the Second half of this book. There are those offenses we could not have avoided. Incest, rape, murder, in other words, acts of sin greater than our attitude. We will be dealing with offenses which were beyond our control to stop or prevent and learn how to overcome the pain of that offense.

"The Grace of Justice" The third session, which is in my first book, "THE GRACE OF JUSTICE"

Learning the great love of God and His need to establish Grace that we might be all he wants us to be. We will learn how God made it possible for us to become qualified to stand in the Justice of God so that we can go to Heaven. We need to comprehend the **'WHY'** Jesus had to come to the cross. We need to understand who we are in sin and how devastating that sin is in our life. It was not a simple ordeal for the Father or Jesus to accomplish salvation for mankind.

Avoidable bitterness – note graph of Mind, Emotion and Will on the CROSS

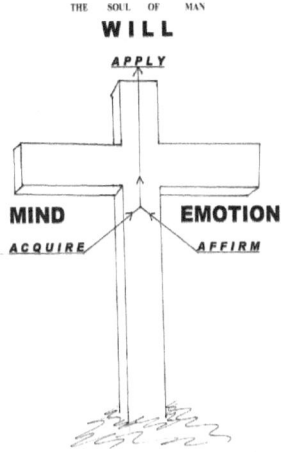

Figure 1: The picture of the soul in the Cross.

Our entanglements with life often come about because of mixed emotions or battles within ourselves. I have learned that more often than not, that when we become offended by what someone has said or done, it was usually while I was in the middle of one of my inner battles. We all fight inner battles within ourselves. When I was fighting that inner battle within myself about rejection, or guilt or what ever the emotion, and someone comes along and makes a silly remark about something in my life, I became offended. Had the person made that same comment or did that same action an hour earlier, when I was not having that inner battle within myself, I would likely have joked back and not given it another thought. But when they made it while I was in battle with myself, I became offended at what they said or did. When I am fighting my inner battle, I learned that I am also in a defensive mood and will take offense to any thing said to me that seems to support the battle I am waging within myself. I was often personally struggling with Carnal feelings of . . . Rejection, Inferior feelings, Inadequate or Unqualified feelings, Feeling Unloved, or Alone while around people. You can see that man's mind has been darkened by sin or to put it truthfully, my mind as darkened by my sin. We find in Romans 8:7 *"Because the carnal mind is enmity against God; for it is not subject to the law of God, nor indeed can be."* At best, our carnal mind is at war with God.

The Will of our Heavenly Father becomes a challenge to our personal Will! We desire to be in total control. As long as our will is in what we believe to be in total control, we are actually at enmity with God the Father. The Holy Spirit has to bring me to a position of knowledge of what Christ has and wants to do through me. Paul in Col. 1:21 writes *"And you, who once were alienated and enemies in your mind by wicked works, yet now He has reconciled (22) in the body of His flesh through death, to present you holy, and blameless, and irreproachable in His sight—"* God understands both who we are and who we can be in Christ. The Father wants to reconcile me through the works of Christ on the Cross - to create a new me. A new me, that will be presented as holy, and blameless and irreproachable in the sight of our Father. God had in mind a plan that we must be brought to the place where we **think** as God thinks! Listen to Paul in Eph 4:22-24 *"that you put off, concerning your former conduct, the old man which grows corrupt according to the deceitful lusts, (23) and be <u>renewed</u> in the spirit of your mind (24) and that you put on the new man which was <u>created</u> according to God, in righteousness and true holiness."* When you come to understand just who you really are, you can get excited about this verse. Think about it. <u>I, in Christ, am created according to God, in righteousness and true holiness!</u>

The renewing of the spirit of my mind comes not by anything I do or can do! It does <u>not</u> come by my performance but through prayer and the Holy Spirit, for Paul writes in Phil. 4:6-7 *"Be anxious for nothing, but in everything by prayer and supplication, with thanksgiving, let your request be made known to God. (7) And the peace of God, which surpasses all understanding, will guard your hearts and minds through Christ Jesus."* Not just praying but also especially praying a prayer of thanksgiving. The Father likes to know you are grateful for all He has done for you. We have a tendency to forget just what Jesus has completed for us on the cross. As we develop a habit of grateful praying, the Father will send to us His peace, a peace beyond anything we could imagine. This will not happen by performing but through meditation on the Word. Listen as the Psalmist gives us instructions on how to renew our minds. Let us read Psalms. 119:1 *"Blessed are the undefiled in the way, who walk in the law (word) of the Lord."* We are to be a people who walk in the way of the Lord. We need to become people who walk applying the Word in our lives. In doing this we will find our lives altering or being renewed to conform to the ways of the Lord. Transformation is a life long process. Listen to John in John 15;5-7 where he quotes Jesus saying, that we are to "abide" in Him and His words are to "abide" in us, then we can accomplish anything we desire. The word 'abide' means to 'settle down in' or 'to make permanent'. When we settle His teaching down or make his teaching to 'settle down' in our life, Jesus and all his promises will become ours! Paul writes in Phil. 1:6 *"being confident of this very thing, that He who has begun a*

good work in you __will complete__ it until the day of Jesus Christ;"
The transformation is both begun and completed by the power of God
and will continue until Jesus comes for us. (I Peter 1:5)

The "Whole" soul of man

In the past, we have been taught to not allow our "feelings" to
govern our "Religion". Well, excuse me, but you cannot separate
your emotions from your faith. We need to understand that this
thinking produces conflict with in our being! My emotions control
my behavior as well as my thinking! I can determine to do or not to
do a certain thing, but if my emotions are not in agreement with my
thinking, or my faith level, then I will find myself yielding to the
control of my emotions. Let us look at ourselves for a bit!

Man's Soul is made up of:

> **Mind** – The desire and ability for analyzing, organizing,
> planning, introspection, researching, learning, intellectual
> energies, and instructing. The mind performs one or more
> of these functions each day.

> **Emotion** - The desire and ability to empathize and respond
> to love, affection, intimacy, gentleness, passion, and
> tenderness. We will and do respond to each of these

emotions each day. Not only do we respond but we yield our behavior and thinking to that response!

Will – The desire and ability for controlling, influencing, leading, conquering, dominating, making decision, expressing, and interacting. We exercise the Will part of our lives based on our emotions in regards to that which our emotions are in agreement to that in our mind.

God has given man a mind that thinks, a will that wants, and an emotion that feels. A man thinks and wants according to what he believes or feels. He may say one thing, but the truth is he will act according to his emotional direction.

Emotion, by not bringing our emotions into alignment with the Holy Spirit and Word of God, we leave the reasoning of our emotions to the "**Carnal Reasoning**" of the old man. Carnal reasoning is under the control or influence of Satan. Carnal reasoning responds to the flesh and not to the Spirit of God.

Far too many of us walk in carnal reasoning rather than in Spiritual or Grace reasoning. We listen to the inner old man rather than to the Spirit of God. We are more accustom to listening to the inner <u>old</u> man, as we have for years, rather than learning to listening to the inner voice of the Holy Spirit as He seeks to direct us each day. We need to train our mind to listen to our spirit, not our spirit to listen to our mind, and we will learn to hear from the Holy Spirit through our spirit, and we will find our conscience more clear on from the Lord.

Lets look again on the next page at God's view of the soul of man on the cross:

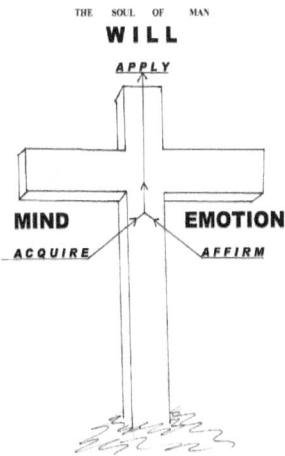

Figure 2: The picture of the soul in the Cross.

.

On the left side of the Cross I have listed the Mind – Note the key word "**ACQUIRE** " listed with the mind on the left side of the Cross.

We must acquire the Word of God in our minds! However, just learning a passage of scripture does not set a pattern of our life. When I was a boy, I heard a man's grandson stand in our church and quote the Bible for over 45 minutes. The trouble is that he is in prison now! He knew the words in his mind but did not know the Word in his heart! We need the Word to be in more than just in our mind.

On the right side of the Cross I have listed Emotion – Note the key word **"AFFIRM** " listed on the right side of the Cross.

What I believe the Holy Spirit has taught me is that we need to get our Emotions aligned up with the Word in our Mind. Now I do not mean in just thinking. I mean that through the Word in our mind we need to get our emotions in agreement with that Word. Our Mind and Emotions need to be in agreement in the Word of God! That takes prayer and submission to the Holy Spirit. Only the Holy Spirit can rightly align our mind and emotions. Romans 12:1-2 (KJV) [1] *I beseech you therefore, brethren, by the mercies of God, that ye present your bodies a living sacrifice, holy, acceptable unto God, which is your reasonable service.* [2] *And be not conformed to this world: but be ye <u>transformed by the renewing of your mind,</u> that ye may prove what is that good, and acceptable, and perfect, will of God.*

Through events in my childhood, my dad set the emotion of rejection in my life. I can remember many a time my dad telling me to run home and hide under the bed so no one would know I was his son! I felt rejected from almost every challenge in my life. I believed that I was not as worthy as other people, especially pastors. I remember one time I attended a pastor's conference and I stood next to the wall away from all other pastors, for I knew or at least I thought I believed that I knew I was not as good as the other pastors. I had a very low esteem of my self worth and felt so rejected. We need to learn that God knows the real us. When I would be challenged to align my emotions with that of what the Word of God teaches, my come back answer was always, "But I know how I *feel*!" I actually believed that my 'feelings' were more accurate than the Word of God! My emotions controlled my actions and my thinking.

Then one day someone challenged me to pit my feelings or emotions against that of the actual Word of God. He taught me that God has a better understanding of my true feelings and that I needed to learn to 'feel' the way the Word of God says that I am to truthfully 'feel"! In particular, I then challenged me to pit my feelings of rejection to that of Ephesians 1:6, "...*made us the accepted of the beloved*." (NKJV), along with Romans 8:1, "*There is therefore now no condemnation to those who are in Christ...*" I was then told that either the Words of God are true or my emotions are a lie, **OR** that the Words of God are a lie and my emotions are true! I cannot have it both ways!

We need to understand a principal of using the Word of God. It is first a seed to be planted. Just because we read the promises of God repeatedly does not mean that the seed has conceived in our heart. Not until the seed of the Word of God becomes conceived in our being, will the Word release its power in our live. We must become pregnant with the promise before it will become birthed in our life. I would read the verse in Ephesians over and over again but I still cried that I knew how I felt. However, after weeks of prayer, one morning the Word impregnated my being and conceived the reality of the Word into my being or spirit. I then began stating out of my mouth the realty that I was made the accepted of the beloved from a conviction as the Word was now conceived in my heart. (See my book, FAITH CHILD OF PROMISE)

How does one know when the Word is conceived in our heart? You can know it is conceived when the Word or seed becomes more real than the issue in your life. Suddenly, the argument of how I felt took on a lesser conviction that the Word of God and the Word became more real than my feelings! Yes, I cried for more than three weeks in my office over this dilemma, as being a pastor I so needed to confess that the Word of God was indeed true. Nevertheless, I still believed I knew how I felt and that my inner feelings were very real, even though they contradicted the Word of God. The thing I had to learn was that my feelings were real, real to my flesh, but not real to the Spirit of God inside me. Once the Word became conceived in my heart, I could finally admit that my emotions were a lie and the Word of God was indeed true! Praise God, once I admitted that the thought I was feeling about rejection was in fact a lie, and was willing to yield to the truth of the Word that I cannot be rejected, I was set free! Did you get that? The Holy Spirit taught me that in Christ Jesus I CANNOT BE REJECTED! What the word teaches is that I do not have to accept rejection or any other put down of sin the Devil wants to throw at me. Paul declared that in fact there could not be any condemnation of guilt, or shame in my life as a born again Saint, (Romans 8:1 (KJV) *"[1] There is therefore now no condemnation to them which are in Christ Jesus, who walk not after the flesh, but after the Spirit."),* especially of rejection in my life. I learned that it was my choice not the enemy's choice to be or not to be rejected and that I had now decided to choose Jesus! What a relief to my self-being! Once I decided to "choose" Jesus over my emotions of rejection, I found the peace I was searching for in my life. I was beginning to learn just who I am in Jesus Christ!

At the top of the Cross is the WILL – And the key word is "**APPLY** ",

Showing that when my mind is filled with the Word of God and my emotions are in agreement with that Word in my Mind, then I could actually apply them to my will to serve my Lord. Listen to the Psalmist in Psalms 119:11 again, *"Thy word have I hid in my heart that I might not sin against God."* Or *"Thy Word (in my mind) have I hid in my heart (my emotions) that I (in my will) might not sin against God"!*

We must "**ACQUIRE THE WORD**" into our minds by reading the Bible. I have come to an amazing discovery and that is that our mind *"leaks"*, therefore we need to continually fill our mind with the Word daily!!! Often we try to acquire the word and then think we can make good decisions for God in our will by just the Word we think we remember in our mind. Nevertheless, then our carnal based emotion circumvents the will and makes a good decision difficult! Because we do not actually look up the actual written promise in the Word and read for ourselves, we then tend to follow our deepest feelings! When we don't reread the Word of God, our carnal mind will begin to alter our memory of the exact words and we will find ourselves misquoting that verse, thereby, changing our understand of the Word of God. Let me demonstrate! I often hear people quoting the word of God saying that God will not **PUT** more on us than we can stand. They are trying to quote I Corinthians 10:13. Let's look at the actual wording of that verse. *"No temptation has overtaken you except such is common to man; but God is faithful, who will not allow you to be tempted beyond what your are able, but with the temptation will also make the way of escape, that you may be able to bear it."* Now, look closely at the written words. Look it up in your personal Bible and show me where it says God puts anything on anyone!!! Because we do not continue to return to read the word, our carnal mind will alter the words and cause us to make an incorrect interpretation!

"Hid in my heart" means that we have through prayer made our feelings or emotions to become the same as the Word in our Mind!!! This means to **"AFFIRM THE WORD"** or make our feeling the same view as the word of God! I must learn to "feel" about me the same as the way God "feels" about me. Paul in Romans 12:3 writes, *"And do not be confirmed to this world (carnal reasoning) but be* *transformed(change of thinking) by the renewing of your mind (Grace reasoning) that you may prove what is that good and acceptable and perfect will of God".(Inserts are mine)* We need to learn to Affirm the last part of that verse as our faith in God's word. Maybe defining a workable definition of the word "faith" would help. **Faith** is the useful application of expressing our daily confidence in God and His Word. Note the word 'confidence' in the definition. This means our emotions must begin to express a daily confidence in God and His word. That means that the Word in our Mind now is set against our feelings (emotions). I had to make a decision that either the Word is truth and my feelings are a lie, or my feelings are true and the Word of God is a lie!!! Go read Habakkuk 3:17, 18. Now you decide just how much you really believe and trust in God?

"So then faith comes by hearing, and hearing by the word of God." I have been told all my life to quote the word of God for help in my troubles. But I must confess that I didn't fully understand how it would work! Allow me to share with you what I have learned. We are to become impregnated with the word of God! When a husband and wife want children, the husband will begin to impregnate the wife with his sperm. The husband will continue to do this until the sperm enters the womb and conception is made. From the conception in the womb, a child will then be produced for their efforts! Well, we are to

read the word of God until a faith child of promise is conceived! This means we are to read the Word of God verbally, so that our own ears will hear the Word and ***then*** it will impregnate our spirit.

As a young boy, even into manhood, I had a real problem of rejection. As a young pastor, I went to a seminar and was challenged to pit my feeling against the Word of God! I had to learn to pit my feelings against the absolute Word of God as opposed to my personal feelings!

The very bottom line is whether, "FREE WILL" is either *My will* or *His will*, and is to be applied in our lives. In Isaiah 14:12-15 noting vs 13-15 **Isaiah 14:13-14 (KJV)** *"[13] For thou hast said in thine heart, I will ascend into heaven, I will exalt my throne above the stars of God: I will sit also upon the mount of the congregation, in the sides of the north: [14] I will ascend above the heights of the clouds; I will be like the most High.* " . . . – we find the words of Satan as he declares, "I Will" or "Pride" or Satan's "Will", as he declares himself equal to or even greater than the Father. That same spirit influences the carnal man today.

In contrast we find John writing in John 1:12 – *"But as many as received Him, to them He gave the right to become children of God, to those who believe in His Name."* The Free will of man is nothing more or less than the power or authority given by God to respond to

Gods will or desire for our life. "We" have the right to make any choice for God that we desire! We can choose to say yes to God or we can choose to reject God. By the same authority, I can choose to say no to Satan as well as to say yes to his luring lies. It is our choice not Satan's! Listen to this principal of life. *"Either I choose Jesus in my situation or Satan will choose my situation for himself."* The choosing is not picking something we like to believe in, but 'choosing' is in the taking or the making something a part of my emotions. Many believe that if they simply do not "choose" Satan then all will be all right. However, we need to understand that not choosing Jesus means we give the enemy the right to choose the situation for himself. The enemy cannot block you from deciding to say "yes" to the will of God. We need to verbally speak that our choice is in the name of Jesus or what I like to do is to declare verbally in the presence of the enemy -- "I choose Jesus" The enemy will try to tell you that you cannot make that choice, but read again **John 1:12 (KJV)** *"[12] But as many as received him, to them gave he power to become the sons of God, even to them that believe on his name:"* , we are given the right to become the children of God (as His child I can make the choice to choose God) by God himself. Not choosing Jesus is in fact giving Satan permission to choose the situation for us!

So then by the Mind or "**ACQUIRING THE WORD**" and the Emotion or "**AFFIRMING THE WORD**" we come into agreement with God so that we can go through the Cross to use our Will to "**APPLY THE WORD**" to make a decision not to sin against God and then do His will.

Look again at the cross analogy. I bring the Word of God into our Mind by reading, but I have only read the Word. The Emotion side of the cross or man means I am to, by the power of the Holy Spirit, allow that word I read into my mind to become a matter of conviction in my emotion or to come into agreement with the Word I read. I must learn to make my emotions the same as the Word of God, by conviction that God knows more how I am to respond emotionally than I do. Isn't that wonderful! Don't get me wrong. It is not easy to achieve. It will take much prayer and probably many tears before the Holy Spirit will be able to renew your Mind and Emotions as one or become in alignment with each other in Word!

WORKSHOP TIME:

Applying this to our lives in areas of carnal feelings.

Scripture: 1 John 2:26-27 *"...The anointing you received from him remains in you, and you do not need anyone to teach you. But as his anointing teaches you about all things and as that anointing is real, not counterfeit—just as it has taught you, remain in him."*

All I can do is present the truth before you, it is the Holy Spirit that teaches you from within to accept and apply that truth. Nuggets of Grace are given to all Saints! You can look at the list of emotions at the end of the first part of this book and find those, which apply, to you. Here are a few to begin…

Inadequate or unqualified or unworthy feelings –

Colossians 2:10 (NKJV) *"[10] and you are complete in Him, who is the head of all principality and power."*,

as well as **2 Corinthians 3:5-6 (NKJV)** *"[5] Not that we are sufficient of ourselves to think of anything as being from ourselves, but our sufficiency is from God, [6] who also made us sufficient as ministers of the new covenant, not of the letter but of the Spirit; for the letter kills, but the Spirit gives life."*

Does God know the real me? Can He really understand how I feel? On the other hand, maybe the problem is that I do not understand God in my life. A little saying I learned as a young man has helped me gain an understanding about my worth compared to what others think of my worth. It goes like this:

As good as you are, and as bad as I am.
I am as good as you are, as bad as I am.

I have learned that I have some good qualities about my life, maybe not the same as yours, but I have them just the same. We need to understand that we all have some good qualities about our life and they will not be the same of other people. Just because you can do something I cannot do, does not make you better than me and for the same reason, just because I can do something better than you does not make me better than you! Because if I will honestly search my life, I will discover that there are some things, I can do better than you can! However bad someone may think I am I have learned that I am loved by God, and that makes me special.

Look   at   the   Graph   (Figure   2)   of   man.

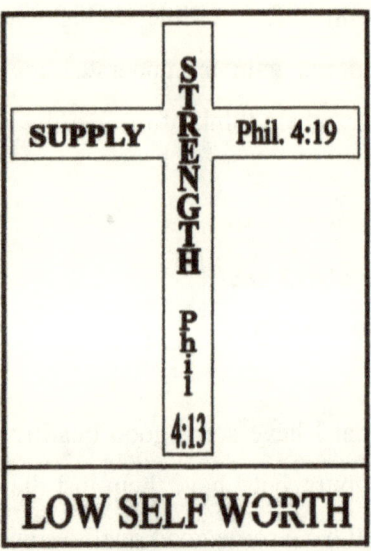

Figure 3 **This is how we view our self worth in relation to what Jesus asks us to accomplish in life.**

The TASK is what God is asking me to do in comparison to how I view my qualification to perform the task!

Consider this: God never called the qualified, but rather qualifies the called!

God will **not** call you to do a new service for Him if you already know how to do the task!

The Lord needs someone who will trust in Him to do the task THROUGH them! Actually, it is what Christ can do <u>through</u> you not what you can do through yourself! The secret is that we are to become his success working through us, not our success, based on our own works! He will supply that which I am short of, to accomplish the task!

My self worth is controlled by my emotions! Note that in the graph that my self worth is often valued very low in relation to the full task Jesus call me to do. I have some knowledge about life, but my emotions control how I apply that knowledge. Let us consider these verses shown on the cross above in figure 2, and how they apply to the challenge of life.

Philippians 4:19 (KJV) "*19 But my God shall supply all your need according to his riches in glory by Christ Jesus.*" – Tell us about the **SUPPLY** of God. When we complain, "I don't have or I need…" I have declared that I do not accept the truth about the supply of God's promises. Our God knew the need long before He asks you to do the task. He has already made available the supply of Grace needed to complete the task available. That need in our life is available through a promise, or you could read this as "*As you have given to me in my distress, God will never suffer you to want without raising up help to you, as he raised you up for help to me.*"

However, we need to learn to walk through that promise to obtain our needs. Walking around the promises will cause us to miss the supply completely. Just as the Israelites walked around the mountain because they would not look at the promises of the Father for their lives, we, have to learn to trust in the Father to know what is best for our lives by trusting in the promises.

I have learned that whatever predicament or challenge that comes my way I am to give God thanks for that problem. Do I mean that I am to be thankful for that problem? No! I am thankful that in the midst of the problem, Christ is with me all the way and I have His promises to overcome and succeed. I have learned that when I give God thanks in the midst of my problem, I am taking the glory away from Satan. Any other attitude about my problem is actually giving Satan permission to use that problem against me! However, when I walk in thankfulness in the midst of my problems, I am giving all the Glory to my Lord and defusing the enemy from using that problem against me!

November of 2007 Wilma and I were driving to Snyder, Texas to do a seminar. About 15 miles short of arriving in Snyder, I looked out my rearview mirror and saw a cloud of smoke coming out of the back of my car. My transmission began slipping and I knew that the transmission had gone bad. It in fact burned up! As I pulled over to the side of the road and parked, Wilma and I immediately held hands and began to give thanks to our precious Father for the protection he had given us. We gave thanks that we were only a few miles from our destination. We knew our God was still looking out for our lives. We committed the situation to his care and gave thanks for his love. We did not want the Devil to get any of the glory for this event. We were not going to give him that satisfaction. The enemy wanted to destroy the seminar, but through our determination and faith to give God all the glory and none to the enemy, we experienced a mighty seminar.

Philippians 4:13 (KJV) "[13] I can do all things through Christ which strengthened me." - The **STRENGTH** of God is given to us to walk in the promises to receive all our supply for the task or challenge. God knew we would have problems walking through His promises, so he gave a supply of Grace and Faith to help us walk through the Promises so we can receive all we need. I see this a little like some of the computer games where you move the man or object and cause it to bump into rewards in order to receive them. If we do not move the man or object forward and cause it to find and bump into the reward, we will miss the supply freely given. Usually the games even give us the power or weapon to achieve the task to find the needed reward. We need to press forward to obtain the Grace God has to strengthen us for all tasks. (Phil. 3:14)

Consider II Cor. 9:8 – *"And God is able to make all grace abound toward you, that you, always having all sufficiency in all things, may have an abundance for every good work."* When we walk through the promises of God and receive the supply of Grace needed to achieve the task, we begin to learn about the all SUFFICIENCEY of God in our life. God had it all planned for success. God always plans for success in our life. When we refuse to walk through the promises of God's Word, we then plan for failure! In walking through the promises of His Word, we gain success. These, supply and strength plus sufficiency, equates unto *"ASSURANCE"* for our lives. I can have the assurance of Gods supply and strength to be all-sufficient for any challenge I face in this life.

Let us look at some of the emotional trials of our lives found in the end of this portion of the book and see what the Word says about how we are to handle each area of our life.

Unrighteousness– I have talked to so many who are striving to become righteous in the eyes of God. I see them doing everything anyone tells them in order to attain righteousness for their life. Many men have the ABC's to achieve righteousness. True to Satan's form, he now has us performing to achieve, and we do it so well! Nevertheless, we believe we are failing in every effort to achieve righteousness for our lives and the truth is, we are failing! As long as we follow the devils plan to perform, we will fail in every effort! (Gal. 5:4) **God has NEVER required us to** *perform* **to attain righteousness!** Note Paul's words in II Cor. 5:21, *"For He (God the Father) made Him (Jesus) who knew no sin to be sin for us, that we might become the righteousness of God (the Father) in Him (Jesus).* (Inserts mine) The Father knew we could not attain righteousness as we were born in sin! We can only perform to obtain for Satan, in Christ we become; we perform in faith because of what Christ had done for us. Read my book "The Grace of Justice" to better understand this. For in Psalms 51:5 we find these words, **"Behold, I was brought forth in iniquity, and in sin my mother conceived me."** I was born a sinner and without the intervention of Jesus Christ's death on the Cross, which includes the shed blood from the stripes, the crown, the nails in his hands and feet, and the spear in the side, I will die a sinner! Note that there is no such thing as a good sinner or a bad sinner. Each of us were born equally a sinner in the eyes of God. One does not become a sinner; we are simply born a sinner! The sins of the soul were sins we committed, and the sin of the Spirit, we inherited. That is why Paul in Romans 3:23 "we have all sinned and come short of the Glory of God."

However, because of the intervention of Jesus Christ on the Cross, which I choose to receive, I am made righteous by Gods Grace. I did not become righteous!!! Rather I was made to be righteous. Did you understand what I just said? I DID NOT BECOME RIGHTEOUS! My spirit is made righteous, not my soul! Nothing of my doing has made me righteous! I do not have to perform to obtain righteousness. Performance is of the Soul and I cannot obtain righteousness of the soul as my righteousness is of the Spirit. I rather just need to recognize that I, as a born again Saint, am righteous! When I was born, I was born into unrighteousness, but when I was born again, I was born into righteousness. I am righteous in my spirit and I am being sanctified daily in my soul.

Rejection - Boy, did I ever fight with this one! I tried everything I knew to get over this and yet everything just made me more rejected! One day when I was about thirteen, I was standing on a street corner in Big Springs, Texas and there were three boys there on the corner. Now, they were not aware that I was there, but I was listening to them as they cut one of the boys to the bone with their words and because of my feelings of rejection, I personally felt the rejection and was hurt by the words spoken to someone I did not even know! I knew then that I had a severe problem. I began praying to God to help me with this heavy problem - I did not wish to carry the burden of rejection of the world on me for the rest of my life.   It was not until I was grown and was the pastor of a church in Snyder, Texas that God began to answer my prayer.

I attended a workshop study dealing with emotions from a Christian prospective.   In this study I was challenged to pit my feelings against the Word! It was suggested that I apply Paul's words in Eph 1:6, *"to the praise of the glory of His grace, by which he has made us ACCEPTED in the Beloved."* to my rejection. This, with Romans 8:1 where Paul says, *"There is therefore now no condemnation to those who are in Christ Jesus, who do not walk according to the flesh, but according to the Spirit.",* I learned that I was made the ACCEPTED in Christ and that I did not need to perform to achieve acceptance. I can only learn to be all that Christ made me to be; therefore, I am righteous. I spent several weeks of tears over this issue. I was still trying to perform for my righteousness or acceptance. I wanted God to be right but I thought I was right also! However, I soon came to the conclusion that God must be correct and I must be wrong! Suddenly I realized that I, in Jesus Christ, could not be rejected. What a burden lifting experience! Rejection is a lie from the enemy and acceptance is a truth from God! I can either choose to believe Satin's lie or God's truth! I learned that rejection is in reality the absence of acceptance. Once I turned on the light of acceptance the darkness of rejection went away!

Consider the following and pit your feelings against the Word!

Where do you view truth!

- Purposeless feelings – John 15:16; Eph 2:10
- Defeated feelings – Romans 8:37
- Unloved feelings – Romans 8:35, 38-39
- Where is God? - Feeling alone –Hebrews 13:5

Grace, rather "GRACE REASONING" was given to us by Christ when we were born again. All these feelings are based on the "feelings" of the old *"CARNAL REASONING"* we had before we were saved. All these and more, we spend much of our Christian effort trying to achieve because of false concepts in our minds! Satan has put many false concepts in our minds to cause us to become misguided in our efforts to serve our Lord. As long as we are basing our faith on 'feelings' we will always be defeated! I had to learn to base my faith on the Word of God, not my feelings. When I did, I began to overcome the false feelings Satan wanted me to focus on.

I would like to share my Personal Vision of being in Heaven:

I was reading in Romans 8:33-34 and it was as if I was in a trance and I seemed to be taken into the heavenlies. I found myself before a veil of which I presumed was the throne of God. I somehow knew that all entities of life had been summoned to attend and no one was excused. All were present, even Satan and his demons.

The Veil began to open and there was the Father and beside Him was my Savior, Jesus Christ, His only Son. The Father stepped forward and began to speak to all present. He spoke, **(33)** *"Who shall bring a charge against God's elect? It is God who justifies. (34) Who is he who condemns? It is Christ who died, and furthermore is also risen, who is even at the right hand of God, who also makes intercession for us."*

WHO? That was the big question asked by the Father! I listened intently and waited to see who would respond to the question of "Who"! However, no one responded! Not even Satan responded to the question of being able to bring a valid charge against any Saint! For it is Christ that Justifies, not our works! Had we as Saints had a part in our salvation, Satan could have rebutted the claim of God, but because it is by the intercession work of Jesus Christ that we are justified and redeemed, not even Satan could rebuttal the claim of the

Father. I knew then and there, that I was secure in the blood of Jesus against the greatest force of evil in existence and that not even the power of Satan could take me out of the Love of Christ! **Romans 8:31-39 (AMP)** *"[1] What then shall we say to [all] this? If God is for us, who [can be] against us? [Who can be our foe, if God is on our side?]*

[32] He who did not withhold or spare [even] His own Son but gave Him up for us all, will He not also with Him freely and graciously give us all [other] things?

[33] Who shall bring any charge against God's elect [when it is] God Who justifies [that is, who puts us in right relation to Himself? Who shall come forward and accuse or impeach those whom God has chosen? Will God, Who acquits us?]

[34] Who is there to condemn [us]? Will Christ Jesus (the Messiah), Who died, or rather Who was raised from the dead, Who is at the right hand of God actually pleading as He intercedes for us?

[35] Who shall ever separate us from Christ's love? Shall suffering and affliction and tribulation? Or calamity and distress? Or persecution or hunger or destitution or peril or sword?

[36] Even as it is written, For Thy sake we are put to death all the day long; we are regarded and counted as sheep for the slaughter.

[37] Yet amid all these things we are more than conquerors and gain a

surpassing victory through Him Who loved us.
[38] For I am persuaded beyond doubt (am sure) that neither death nor
life, nor angels nor principalities, nor things impending and
threatening nor things to come, nor powers,
[39] Nor height nor depth, nor anything else in all creation will be able
to separate us from the love of God which is in Christ Jesus our
Lord."

I now began to understand just who I am in Christ! This means
that because we do not understand nor accept who we are in Christ,
then and only then does Satan have power over us. He will use the
Word we do not know, understand, and accept against us. However,
when I learn in the Word just who I am, I become the victor.

The Father sat back on the throne and the Veil closed. However,
I was still present in the vision. I looked around and I found myself
standing over all the servants of Satan. They were in a panic and I
could hear them complaining to Satan. "What will we do now?" they
were asking. "How can we deal with the Saints if we cannot put guilt,
or shame, or un-forgiveness on them?" "How can we bring
condemnation on them if the Grace of God has blocked the Saints
from all condemnation?" I looked, and Satan was standing there and
was smiling! I heard him tell this to his demon servants, *"It does not*
matter! It does not matter!" He continued, *"Because the Saints do*

not understand who they are in Christ Jesus, all you have to do is to point your finger at them and bring an accusation against them, <u>and they will do the rest</u>!" "<u>They will take the condemnation upon themselves!</u>" Satan knew that while neither he nor his demons could place condemnation on the Saints, he knew that we as Saints could place condemnation on ourselves! Satan is indeed the accuser of the brethren! Eleanor Roosevelt once said something to the effect, "No one can place condemnation upon us without our consent!" Now, tell me again, where did your condemnation come from???

Because we do not know and understand who we are in Christ Jesus, we will take up that accusation and place it upon ourselves, the very condemnation that Christ nailed to the Cross, freeing us from any condemnation! Any and all condemnation, past present and future, we are carrying from our time in sin is nailed to the cross and no longer belongs to us as well as any sin to be committed in the future. Because we refuse to acknowledge who we are in Jesus, we will listen to the lying accusation that the demons speak to us and we think that they are speaking truth! We will now believe we owe the debt again. Listen to the mind trick Satan speaks to us as opposed to that which God teaches:

YOU CANNOT ACQUIRE RIGHTEOUSNESS!

I fail to understand that according to the Word I am made righteous by the blood of Jesus. While in the old man, the carnal self, I would seek to acquire righteousness. I would seek many ways to "turn over that new leaf to acquire righteousness". Yet, with each leaf I turned over, there was always another leaf to turn over, not only that, but we are now trying to live on the bad side of the leaf! There was always a friend to tell me how to become more righteous, or the church to inform and lead me into righteousness. I found my self, working myself to death, for something that I never seemed to be able to obtain. All the time I never did understand a basic principal in life.

YOU CANNOT ACQUIRE THAT YOU ALREADY HAVE!

Let me ask you a question and I want you to answer the question. As a male, what can you do to become a male? Alternatively, a female, what can you do to become a female. Think about this silly question very seriously. Go on and answer the question honestly! What can you do to become what you *already* are? Why don't we work as hard to become a male or female, as we do to become righteous? Why? Because common sense tells you that, you already are what you are. You cannot become what you already are! Now do not hand me that deceptive argument that some are born in the wrong body. A simple blood test will prove what your body really is and every soul is born into the correct body! The DNA of a butterfly is the same as it was as a caterpillar. Listen to the Word and understand that you cannot become righteous, as in Christ, you are already righteous!

YOU CANNOT ACQUIRE ACCEPTANCE!

When I came to understand who I am in Christ, I then begin to understand that I am already made the accepted of the Beloved! In Christ Jesus, I do not have to accept rejection! The enemy will try to speak rejection toward me, but I know that I cannot be condemned! God loves me just the way he made me through the blood of Christ, as I was created in Christ Jesus the way God planned from the beginning! Now that I realize the truth of God's word, that I cannot be rejected, I now live more at peace within myself and with others! If I have truly surrendered myself to Jesus, then I no longer believe that I am being rejected. I now know that they (the enemy working through others) are rejecting Jesus Christ and not me! Did you understand what I just said? When anyone or anything begins to reject you, if you understand who you are in Christ, the rejection is really of Jesus Christ and NOT you! When I feel rejection coming toward me, I need to pass it on to Jesus and tell him, "Lord, see what they are trying to do to you!"

YOU CANNOT ACQUIRE THE STATE OF BEING ADEQUATE!

I now know that in Christ, I was made complete and anything else I need, God has promised to supply. Everything I need to accomplish whatever task He calls me to do, God has furnished! If it is knowledge, He will supply knowledge, if wisdom, He will supply wisdom, if strength, He Promises to supply all the strength I need to accomplish his will. I just need to learn to trust in his SUPPLY! (Phil 4:19)

YOU CANNOT ACQUIRE A PURPOSE IN LIFE!

Our Father, through Christ Jesus, declared that I from the beginning of time was created unto good works and that God will accomplish his creation in me! (Ephesians 1:3-6; 2:10)   Paul in Philippians 1:6 states, *"being confident (persuaded) of this very thing, that He who has begun a good work in you will complete it until the day of Jesus Christ."* God does not create junk, therefore, I am not junk. I may be coming out of junk, but once in Christ I am no longer junk! I am created in the image of God and created unto His good works! I was created with a purpose in life. My task, if accepted, is to live that purpose. In the word, I am given purpose. Many today are 'trying to find themselves'. Well, while they are falsely looking for themselves in the world, I have found my self in Christ. I am to be living that purpose, and I learn the daily purpose of my life is by living the Word in my life. The secret is to accept His purpose taught in the Word.

YOU CANNOT ACQUIRE THE LOVE OF GOD!

Most of us waste our lives "performing" to get someone to love us.   We perform to *EARN* love from family, from friends, and sometimes from those we really do not care much about. In addition, we then begin applying that same act of "performing" in an attempt to earn God's love. "I might think that maybe if I live this way or that way, God will love me more!"   Man thinks in terms of loving someone more. I sometimes will say to my granddaughter, Mikayla, I love you, to which she replies', "I love you more" To which I reply I love you double more and so on… God simply loves man as he is and there cannot be 'more' love of God. The only way to experience more love of God is in how much we are willing to accept of God's love in the first place. His love never changes; it is the capacity in our heart that measures the Love of God. It is not God loving us more, but us choosing to receive more of His love already given. As long as we view our Heavenly Father on the same level as earthly fathers, we will always strive to perform for His love. God the Father is not an earthly father and is not required to love as an earthly father. He comes from the place of prefect love. We need to learn that God's love is unconditional, complete and was initiated from the beginning of time; – it is we who place conditions on being loved!

We place conditions on each other to gain love. Funny how it never works the way we imagined! The success of performing for love exists only in our daydreams! The love found in our daydreams is a product of our imagination. We are searching for an imagined love and cannot find it as we are always searching for that which only exists in our minds as created by Satan. Is that what you want, love found only in your imagination? That love fabricated in our imagination, when tested against life, fails miserably. That is one reason why we believe so many people do not love us! They could not measure up to the love standard fashioned in our imagination, so we concluded that they must not really love us, when in fact they may be really trying to love us and it is we who are not functioning in the real acceptance of love! Because they do not measure up to the imagined love of our mind, we reject their offer of love. Real love is brought into being in the exercise of faith or the confidence in Jesus Christ as the Lord of our hearts. Only in Christ can we experience perfect love.

YOU CANNOT ACQUIRE
WHAT YOU ALREADY HAVE!!!!

If you are married, turn to your mate and ask them if they will marry you! Turn to your mother and ask her if she will again give birth and be your mother! They cannot give you what you already have. Yet, we spend out lives searching for that we already possess. The difficultly is not in discovering life, but acknowledging that we already hold life. The "Old Man" within us lies to us in that we must perform to attain, while the "Spirit" within us declares that we already have attained, and that we need to learn to see ourselves as having attained all in life given by Christ! So…I repeat:

WE NEED TO LEARN THAT WE CANNOT ACQUIRE WHAT WE ALREADY HAVE!

I <u>need</u> to acknowledge that God has **ALREADY** given all I am to me and that I only need to adjust my emotions or "feelings" or "way of thinking" to accept that <u>What God says about me is the true ME</u>! I need to come to a full understanding of life in Christ. That is,

EITHER, MY EMOTIONS ARE TRUE AND GOD'S WORD IS A LIE,

Or

MY EMOTIONS ARE A LIE AND GOD'S WORD IS TRUE!

One statement or the other is to become the foundation of my life. We cannot believe both! I know as I have tried. The workshop I attended challenged me to pit my deepest emotion trial against the Word of God. My come back to all who tried to counsel me was that,

"But I know how I feel!" I had a rejection problem in the worst way and I was in denial. As friends would try to share with me the wonderful truths of the Word of God as in Eph. 1:6 where Paul wrote, *" ...which He has made (bestowed grace upon us) us accepted in the Beloved or Jesus Christ my Savior."* He also reminded me of Romans 8:1 in that *"There is therefore NOW no condemnation to those who are in Christ Jesus, who do not walk according to the flesh, but according to the Spirit."* I acknowledge the Word as the Word of God, but I insisted that my feelings were just as real! That wonderful workshop challenged me to pit the two concepts against each other to learn that only one could be true! For a little over three weeks, I cried in my office as I wrestled over the two concepts in my mind and heart. I wanted so much to authenticate the Word as truth, but then my emotions would rise up and became more genuine than the Word of God. Strange how the emotions of my mind would make ineffective that which I knew in my heart to be the truth of the Word of God. I knew both could not be true, especially in my life, not as a pastor of a church. I finally began to pray and ask the Holy Spirit to help me resolve the two concepts wrestling over and over in my mind and heart. As I prayed, I soon learned that:

WHAT GOD SAYS I AM, I AM!

WHAT GOD SAYS I HAVE, I HAVE!

I must learn to **THINK** of me as the Word of God **THINKS** of me in order to be and have what God has for me in life! I had to accept the truth that my Father in Heaven sees me differently than the way I think of myself.

I must learn to experience the way God thinks about me! Indeed, I had to have a change of judgment about me and about what God thinks about me! I had to come into agreement with Him; rather I had to come into agreement of His concept of me as opposed to trying to make God come into agreement with my feelings. I had to learn that His view of me was accurate, not the thoughts I had about me! I had to learn that it is only through the Cross of Jesus that I can achieve these things – Gal. 2:20 *"I have been crucified with Christ; it is no longer I who live, but Christ lives in me; and the life which I now live in the flesh I live by faith in the Son of God, who loved me and gave Himself for me."*

Note the part *"Christ lives in me"*! We tend to forget that as a Saint it is Christ living in us not us in Christ! The carnal mind states "I live in Christ", while the grace mind states "Christ lives in me!" I cannot fail when I remember that Christ living in me cannot fail. It is only when I see myself living in Christ that I fail, as the emphases is now on me! I believe I am in control. When I walk, seeing myself in

Christ, I am looking at what I am doing, and will always stumble. When I am allowing Christ to walk in me, I am looking at Christ and trusting in his steps and then and only then do I succeed.

How this relates to Bitterness and Forgiveness

I now understand that many of the offenses we feel from others actually <u>come</u> from within us. I make the offense against ME! When I can see it in its reality, I will see it is personally against Jesus. However, we center in on the belief that the offense is against ourselves. When we do that, his or her offense becomes much bigger than any sin we have ever committed against anyone else.

Their offense is a Sin! Right? When we center in on the judgment of sin of others, we begin to measure how great a sin was committed against us. Now that is the problem, when we center in on the judgment of that sin committed against us. Now ask yourself this question. Have I ever committed a personal sin against the Son of Almighty God? Be honest! Then we have to ask how great that sin was? Because of your sin and my sin, Jesus had to come down from Heaven, He had to become a man, He then had to became obedient to the Cross, so that he could experience death, just so you and I could have our sins redeemed and forgiven! Note that my sin against Jesus brought about condemnation for my life. Now is that what the sin someone commits against you brings to your life?

In Eph. 4: 32…Paul writes," *just as Christ forgave you…* " We all too quickly forget that we sinned against Jesus and He forgave us. Paul reminds us that we are to "judge" others sins against us in that same spirit of forgiveness we received from Jesus. In Col. 3:13 Paul reminds us *"Bear with each other and forgive whatever grievances you may have against one another. Forgive as the Lord forgave you!"* I need to learn to look at my brother through the eyes of Jesus rather than the eyes of the enemy! Sometimes we need to learn to "overlook" what someone has done rather than to judge him or her. Remember the words of Peter in 1 Peter 4:8 *"…love will cover a multitude of sins".* I need to learn to take the *grievances* I have against my brother or sister and simply forgive them. How? By surrendering them to Jesus, remembering that Jesus has forgiven you of the grievances you committed against him. Note that it is the person that is forgiven, not the sin! I also need to remember it is not me in Christ but Christ in me!

Go to Matt: 18:23-35 and read about the Servant forgiven by his master and then see how that servant chooses not to forgive his servant. The debt owed by this servant was real! However, the master forgave the debt owed by his servant and the debt owed to that servant was also real! Nevertheless, this servant failed to forgive as he was forgiven.

Note that in **Ephesians 4:32 (KJV)** "...*[32] And be ye kind one to another, tenderhearted, forgiving one another, even as God for Christ's sake hath forgiven you.* " ... and also in **Colossians 3:13 (KJV)** "**[13] Forbearing one another, and forgiving one another, if any man have a quarrel against any: even as Christ forgave you, so also do ye.** " ... The Word states that as Jesus forgave you, you are to forgive!!! If Jesus forgave you, where do you come up with the audacity to not forgive? What if God the Father did to you what the master did to the servant all because he failed to extend the same forgiveness. Read 1 Peter 4:12-16 and learn that we are to not question the trials, but rather to rejoice that we can walk through them in Christ!

We were never told that living for Jesus would not present trials! We are having problems because we are self-centered! We need to remember Peter when the religious leaders told him that he was to never to talk about Jesus in public again and if he did, he would be severely beaten! His position was that of who else can we speak of but Jesus! We with Peter must consider all things we experience worth it all in Christ. I need to learn that nothing in life is done to me, but in reality done against Christ living in me.

Also look at Paul and Silas while in the third level down in the dungeon, filled with sewage of the town and yet sang praise songs! Tell me again about what someone said or did that was so great!!!

Consider the scripture Matt. 6::14 *"For if you forgive men when they sin against you, your heavenly Father will also forgive you.* ***But if you do NOT forgive men their sins, you Father will not forgive your sins."*** – If you do not forgive, you will not be forgiven! Who told you that you had a right to be bitter? Who told you had a right to feel that way toward someone? Only Satan teaches that we have a right to be bitter or angry with someone. We need to look to God's standard to learn possibly the 'why' of the conflict. We need to learn to forgive the person and allow Jesus to deal with what others have done. Many times God allows this conflict to come your way to reveal or mirror a crack or flaw in your character giving you the opportunity to correct the problem and thereby grow in Christ.

LET'S DEAL WITH BEING OFFENDED

What about when someone says something offensive, does something to offend us, or fails to do something we think has wronged us? If our "feelings" were lined up with the Word in our heart, we would have a different perspective of the wrong done to us.

If we could see the issue as the Word sees the issue, we would not have been hurt! If I love my brother/sister, I will overlook that action. God teaches that love covers a multitude of sins! Try this on for size! I cannot love God and hate my brother/sister at the same time. (**1 John 4:20 (AMP)** *[20] If anyone says, I love God, and hates (detests, abominates) his brother [in Christ], he is a liar; for he who does not love his brother, whom he has seen, cannot love God, Whom he has not seen.*

Because I became offended and bitter, I am now **more** wrong than the offender! Therefore, I need to go ask for forgiveness for being offended even if I am 100% in the right. Look in Romans 12:20 – 21, *"If your enemy is hungry, feed him; if he is thirsty, give him something to drink. In doing this, you will heap burning coals on his head!"* When you do it God's way they now must take the "defensive position"

Ok, let's deal with being offending by someone. Even if they meant what they did or said at the time, it is we, ourselves, who must deal with the guilt! We must make a decision: Which one of us will be the bigger Saint?

If I am righteous then I must repent and change my "feelings" from bitterness to love, from self serving to the Lordship of Jesus Christ. Then I must go to that person and ask for forgiveness for allowing bitterness to enter my heart for what they did or said to me. I had no right to allow bitterness into my heart as this makes my unforgiveness the greater sin or offence than the offence that I felt was done to me. This is against all carnal standards, but totally in line with God's standards! I am to become the bigger Saint!

Many today practice a worldly theology of what I call, "Justified unforgiveness"! I hear this expressed in this way, people will tell me that they love Jesus with all their heart and that He means everything to them, but no way in hell will they forgive so and so! They are practicing justified unforgiveness. This is a teaching given only by Satan. They believe that because they "love" Jesus, they have the right to forgive or not to forgive, depending on the situation. I hear, "But you don't know what they did to me!" or "You don't know what they said to me!" What they are in reality telling me is that either they have forgotten what Jesus did for them or they do not believe they did anything that bad to Jesus Christ, the Son of God! Carnality has a way of making us forget just what Jesus has done for us. There is no greater sin committed, than the sin committed to Jesus by rejecting Him! **John 3:18 (KJV)** *[18] He that believeth on him is not condemned: but he that believeth not is condemned already, because he hath not believed in the name of the only begotten Son of God.* The only sin that keeps a spirit and soul condemned to hell is rejecting

Jesus Christ as personal Lord and Saviour; this sin keeps one condemned to Hell, not his carnal works! (see my book "The Grace of Justice) Moreover, either every one of you are rejecting Him right now, or at one time in your life you have rejected Jesus! Yet, God the Father loves and forgave you! Jesus Christ is the one who took the 39 stripes on his back for your sin, indeed the scriptures teach that without the shedding of blood there can be no remission of sin! Note the reference in *Hebrews 9:22 (KJV)* *"²² And almost all things are by the law purged with blood; and without shedding of blood is no remission."* And then He died on the cross to pay the ultimate price for your sin, and yet, HE REDEEMED AND FORGAVE YOU! Let's read that in **Isaiah 53:4-6 (KJV)** *"⁴ Surely he hath borne our grief's, and carried our sorrows: yet we did esteem him stricken, smitten of God, and afflicted.*

⁵ But he was wounded for our transgressions, he was bruised for our iniquities: the chastisement of our peace was upon him; and with his stripes (the shedding of blood) we are healed. (of our spiritual sin against God) [inserts mine] ⁶ All we like sheep have gone astray; we have turned every one to his own way; and the LORD hath laid on him the iniquity of us all." His blood was shed for our iniquities or as we today better understand it, our sins. Not just any sin, but designates the sin man commits against God. The consequences of iniquity was predicted in **Genesis 2:17 (KJV)** [17] *But of the tree of the knowledge of good and evil, thou shall not eat of it: for in the day that thou eat thereof you shall surely die.* Death was the curse of the sin of iniquity against the Father and the curse of death came upon Adam and Eve as the Father predicted. And they then passed the curse of death to all future generations of mankind. It took not only the obedience of Christ to the Cross, but the death of Jesus on the Cross to satisfy the curse of death. Only in the resurrection of Jesus from the grave, becoming victorious over death, could Jesus offer new life to all humankind. Had Jesus not taken the stripes on his back, the crown of thorns on his head and the spear into his side, no blood would have been shed for the remission of our sins and our sins would not have been forgiven!

Forgiveness is not an option! This restores respect or brings respect of you to that person as well as to yourself. Being bitter does not show or command any respect on our part nor does it show or command any respect from their part! We can read about that in Psalms 51:1-13 (you read). As a Saint, first, I must acknowledge my sin and then ask for forgiveness for that sin, both from God and from the one offended.

Ask yourself, "How important is walking in the Forgiveness of God" to you?" Is it important enough to forgive anything someone has said or done? According to the Word of God, there is no one worth walking in bitterness for! If we want to receive forgiveness in our life, we must forgive! Again, look at my Seminar motto.

"TO WALK IN FORGIVENESS
YOU MUST WALK IN FORGIVENESS"

How important is walking in God's Love to you? It is important enough to love that person because you choose to walk in Agape Love and not with carnal feelings? What means more to you – your Pride or your Forgiveness? Do you believe you deserve to walk in Christ's Forgiveness and Love? Then...

FORGIVENESS IS NOT AN OPTION!

To not forgive, you have committed the greater SIN!!! You allowed their action or word to create bitterness in you! This is not allowed of a Saint of God. Allowing yourself to become bitter, you are NOW in need of asking THEM to forgive you for being bitter toward them! Now, you need to go to them and ask their forgiveness for you becoming bitter!!!

<u>Some of you reading this right now, have a need to go to someone and ask them to forgive you for being offended at something you thought they did. How real are you willing to become to walk in God's forgiveness?</u>

You can blame them all you want to, but you are the Saint or child of God, which means you have the greater responsibility to do what the Word of God teaches. Your example might be the very spark to turn someone's heart around and might cause him or her to repent to Jesus. On the other hand, is it that you still feel it is all about you! As long as you feel it is about you, then you are living in the old carnal man and not in the Spirit of God! Your life and my life is about bringing praise to Jesus, not satisfying self. However, far too many of us are more concerned about pleasing ourselves, than by doing something to bring praise to Jesus. I feel that far too many of the church members today have lost their first love, which is of pleasing Jesus Christ. We live as if life is about us!

Following pages are emotional trials of life, I believe you can find yourself somewhere in them! Search and find the scripture to put into your mind then to affirm in our heart.

EMOTIONAL TRIALS

ADULTRY
Exodus 20:14
Prov. 6:20-35\
Heb. 13:4
Matt 5:27-30

ALCOHOL ABUSE
Prov. 20:1
Prov. 23:29-35
Eph. 5:15
I Cor. 6:9,10
I Cor. 6:15,19-20

ANGER
Prov. 14:17,20
James 1:19,20
Gal 5:19-25
Eph. 4:26
Col. 3:8
Rom. 6:11-14

ANXIETY
Matt 6:25-34
Phil 4:6-7
Matt 28:10
I Pet 5:6,7

ASSUSRANCE OF SALVATION
Matt. 24:35
John 5:24
John 6:37
John 10:28
John 20:31
Rom 10:9-10
I John 5:13
I John 4:13-16
II Tim 1:12
I Pet 1:3-5
Rom 8:16,17

BITTERNESS
Gal 5:19
Eph 4:31
Heb 12:15
I John 2:9-11
I John 3:15
Rom 12:9-14,17-21

BLAME SHIFTING
Gen 3:21,13
Prov. 19:3
Matt 7:1-5
John 8:10,11

BROODING
Prov 15:13

Psalms 37
Is. 61:2,3
I Pet 1:6-9
Phil 4:8

CHASTISEMENT(GOD'S)
Psalms 119:67-76
Heb. 12:5-11
Is. 28:17
I Cor. 10:13
Rev. 3:19,20

CHILD ABUSE
Prov 19:11
Luke 17:13
I Cor. 13:4-7
Eph. 4:26,27
Col. 3:2,8
Gal. 5:22,23
I Cor. 10:13
James 4:7
Jude 24,25
Psalms 127:3

CHILDREN(Salvation)
Psalm 127:3
Matt. 19:13-15
Gen. 17:7
Acts 2:39
Acts 16:31

CHRISTIAN FELLOWSHIP
Matt. 18:20
John 13:34
Acts 2:42
Acts 2:42
Heb. 10:25
I John 1:3

CHURCH
Eph. 4:3-6:1:20-23
Rom. 12:4-8
I Cor 1:10,11
I Cor. 12
Psalms 84
Heb. 10:25
I John 2:19
Matt. 28:18-20

CHURCH DISCIPLINE
Gal. 6:1
James 5:19,20

II Cor. 2:7,8
I Cor 5:11
II Thes. 3:14
Rev. 2:2, 14-16

COMFORT
Psalms 23
Psalms 139:1-3
Rom. 8:18,31,38,39
II Cor 1:3,4
Psalms 55:22
Psalms 34:15-19
John 14:16-18
II Thes. 2:16,17

COMPULSIVENESS
I Cor 9:24-27
I Cor 10:13
Gal 5:19-23
Rom 6:11
John 15:5
Rom 6:12,13
I Cor 9:26,27

CONFIDENCE
Psalms 27:3
Prov 14:26
Gal 6:9
Phil 4:13
Heb 10:35

CONTENTMENT
Phil 4:11-13
Heb 13:5
Prov 23:4,5
I Tim 6:6-10

CONVETING
Ex 20:17
Col 3:5
Prov 4:11-13
Phil 4:11-13
Heb 13:5

CULTS
Psalms 119:104
Mark 13:21-23
I John 4:1-3
IICor 11:13-15
Deut 13:1-5
Deut 18:20-22

DANGER
Psalms 91
Psalms 23:4
Psalms 24:7
II Chron 20:17

EMOTIONAL TRIALS

DEATH
Psalms 23:4
Rev 14:13
Ii Cor 5:1-8
John 14:1-4
I Cor 15:50-57
I Thes 4:13-18
Heb 9:27

DEPRESSION
Psalms 32:3,4
Psalms 32:1,2,5,61
II Cor 4:8,9
Psalms 34:17,18
Psalms 55:22
Psalms 27:14

DESPAIR
Haggai 2:4
Jer 32:17
Is 40:29; 51:6-8
Psalms 46:
Psalms 119:1,16
James 1:12
II Thes 3:3
Psalms 100:5
Eph 1:18

DESPERATE
Psalms 30:5
Psalms 42:11
Psalms 34:18
Psalms 126:5
Psalms 40:1,2
John 10:10

DISAPPOINTMENT
Psalms 43:5
Psalms 55:22
John 14:27
II Cor 4:8,9

DISCOURAGEMENT
Psalms 27:14
John 14:1,27
Heb 4:16
I John 5:11
Phi :6
Deut 33:27
II Kings 6:16

DIVORCE
Mal 2:113-16
Matt 5:31,32

Is 41:20
Is 54:17

Matt 19:4-6
Rom 7:1-3
I Cor 7:10-35
Is 43:18,19

DRUG ABUSE
Prov 20:1
Prov 23:29:35
Eph 5:15-18
I Cor 6:9,10,15, 19,20
I Cor 5:11
Prov 23:19,20
Prov 25:28

ENEMIES
Prov 24:17,18
Luke 6:27-37
Psalms 18:47-48
Psalms 44:5-7
Phil 4:13
Luke 23:34
Acts 7:59,60
Rom 12:14,19-21

ETERNAL LIFE
John 11:23-26
John 3:3-8, 15-18
John 5:24
John 10:25-29

EVIL DESIRES
I Peter 1:14-16
Gal. 5:16
Rom 8:5-8
Rom 13:14
Titus 2:11,12

FAITH (IN GOD)
Heb 10:28; 11:1,6
Rom 10:17
Eph 2:8,9
Rom 4:19-22
Mark 9:23
Rom 5:1,2
II Cor 5:7
Eph 6:16
Matt 9:29
Matt 21:21
Rom 1:17

FEAR
Rom 8:15
II Tim 1:7
Heb 13:5,6
Psalms 27:1
Rom 8:31,38,39
Psalms 91

I John 4:18
Psalms 4:8
Psalms 28:7

FORGIVENESS FOR SINS(GOD'S FORGIVENESS)
Psalms 32:3-5
Psalms 51:1-17
Matt 6:12
Psalms 86:4-7
I John 1:9
Prov 28:13,14
I Cor 6:9-11

FORGIVING OTHERS
Matt 6:12-15
Matt 18:21-35
I Peter 4:8
Gal 6:1
II Cor 5:11
Rom 12:14,21
Col 3:12,13

FREEDOM FROM DEMONIC BONDAGE
Deut 18:10-13
Eph 6:12
Matt 8:28,32
Acts 5:16
Gal 5:19-23
Rom 10:13
I Cor 12
Mark 16:9-20
Mark 1:23-27
Luke 8:2
Matt 18:18
Luke 10:17-20
James 4:7-10

FRIENDSHIPS
Prov 17:17
Prov 18:24
Eccl 4:9-10
Prov 27:6
I Cor 15:33
John 15:14-18

GIVING
Luke 21:1-4
I Cor 16:1,2
II Cor 9:6,7
II Cor 8:1-5
Luke 6:38
Prov 19:17
Prov 3:9,10

2 of 6 Ministries of Forgiveness

EMOTIONAL TRIALS

Prov 11:24,25
Mal 3:10,11
Matt 25:40

GOSSIP
Psalms 19:14
Eph 4:29
Prov 15:1
Prov 11:11-13
Prov 12:18
Prov 17:27,28
Prov 29:19
James 1:19
Psalms 141:1

GUIDANCE
Psalms 32:8
Is 30:21;58:11
John 16:13
Prov 3:5,6
Palms 48:14-17
Psalms 25:9
Is 42:16
John 10:27
James 1:5
Psalms 119:59,105

GUILT
Rom 3:19-23
Rom 6:23
I John 1:9
Matt 4:17
Is 44:22
Rev 2:4,5
Rom 8:1
Psalms 32:1

HELP AND CARE
II Chron 16:9
Psalms 34:7
Psalms 37:5
Heb 4:16
Is 50:9
Is 54:17
Heb 14:6

HOMOSEXUALITY
Gen 19:4,5,24,25
II Pet 2:6-10a
June 6
Rom 1:26,27
Rom 6:11-14,22
I Cor 6:9,10,11
I Tim 1:10-11

HOPE
Psalms 42:5
Psalms 145:5,6
Psalms 146:5
I Pet 1:3
Psalms 33:18
Lam 3:26
Rom 5:2

HUSBAND/WIFE REATIONSHIP
Gen 2:18,24
Eph 5:21-33
Col 3:18,19
I Pet 3:7
I Tim 3:4
I Tim 2:11-14
Prov 12:4; 18:22
Heb 13:4
I Cor 7:2

I CAN'T; UNQUALIFIED
Phil 3:13
Phil 3:19
Col 2:10
II Cor 12:9

INCEST/MOLESTATION
Lev 18:6,29
Lev 20:11,12,14,17
Mark 6:17,18
I Cor 5:1,5,6
I Cor 6:13-18; 7:2
Rom 13:14
Prov 2:16-19
Prov 6:20;7:27
Rom 1:18-32

INSOMNIA
Psalms 3:5; 4:8
Psalms 127:2
Prov 3:24-26
Matt 11:28
Is 26:3
Is 29:10

JESUS IS SAVIOR
Matt 1:1
Luke 19:10
John 3:16,18
John 14:6
Acts 4:12
Rom 5:8
Eph 1:7
I John 5:12

JUDGEMENTAL/ CRITICISM
Matt 7:1,2
John 8:1-12
Mark 11:25
Luke 6:31
I Cor 4:3-5
Rom 14:4

LAZINESS
II Tim 2:15
I Cor 10:31
Eph 4:28
I Thes 4:11,12
II Thes 3:6-15

LIVING THE CHRISTIAN LIFE
John 15:7
Psalms 119:11
II Cor 5:17
Col 2:6
I Pet 2:2
I John 1:7

LONELINESS
Psalms 27:10
Matt 28:20
Heb 13:5
I Pet 5:7
Psalms 31:7
Psalms 103:13

LOVE (GOD'S LOVE)
John 3:16
John 15:9
Rom 5:8
Rom 8:38,39
I John 3:1

LOVING AND SERVING OTHERS
I John 4:9-11,21
I Pet 1:22
I Pet 4:8
I Cor 13:4-7
Rom 12:9,10
John 13:14,15,34
Matt 20:26-28
Matt 25:35,36,40
Gal 5:13-15
Gal 6:10
Mat 5:43-48
Rom 12:20,21

LOVING GOD
Deut 6:4-7

EMOTIONAL TRIALS

Matt 22:37-39
John 14:23,24
II Cor 5:14,15

LUST
Matt 5:27-30
Eph 4:22-24
Eph 5:3-7
James 1:15
Titus 2:11,12
Rom 13:14
Eph 2:3-5
I Pet 1:14-16
Gal 5:16

LYING
Prov 4:24;12:22
Prov 19:9
Eph 4:25
John 8:44
James 3:1-12

MARRIAGE
Gen 2:18-25
Eph 5:22-33;6:4
I Pet 3:7
I Tim 2:11-1;3:4
I Pet 3:1-4,7
Matt 19:11,12
Mark 10:10:7-9
I Cor 7:9-14,39
Col 3:18,19
II Cor 6:14
Heb 13:4

MENTAL ILLINESS
Is 26:3
Matt 17:13-18
Deut 28:15,28
Luke 4:18,19
Rom 4:9
I Tim 1:7
Gal 3:13
Phil 2:1-13

OBEDIENCE
Psalms 119:1-4
John 14:15,21
John 15:10-17
Prov 13:13
Luke 11:28
Matt 7:21
I John 5:2,3
Matt 6:24
I John 3:22

OCCULT
Ex 22:18

Rev 21:8
Luke 4:18,19
Luke 10:17-19
Eph 1:17-23
Mark 16:17
Matt 16:19;18:18
Gal 5:19-21

OVERCOMING EVIL (WHEN OTHERS WRONG YOU)
Matt 18:15-17
Rom. 12:14-21
Prov. 20:22
Prov. 24:28,29
I Pet 3:8,9
Matt 5:38-47
I Thes 5:15

OVERCOMING SIN
John 8:24-36
II Pet 1:3
Phil 2:13
Eph 4:22-24
Col 3:9,10
Phil 3:13
Heb 12:1
I Cor 6:12
II Tim 3:16,17
Rom 8:1-7
Gal 5:16

OVERCOMING TEMPTATION
Matt 26:41
I Cor 10:13
Phil 1:6
II Thes 3:3
II Pet 2:9

PEACE
Matt 11:28-30
Rom 5:1
John 14:27
John 16:33
Luke 7:36-50
Psalms 4:8
Rom 8:6; 14:17-19
Gal 5:22,23
Phil 4:6,7

PERSECUTION
Matt 5:10-11
Mark 10:22
Acts 9:16
II Tim 3:12
I Pet 2:20

PRAYER
Matt 6:9-15
Heb 4:14-16
I Pet 5:6,7
Phil 4:6-7
I Thes 5:17,18
James 1:6
James 5:13-16
Psalms 34:15-18
Luke 6:12;11:9-13

PRIORITIES
Matt 6:24,33
Prov 23:4,5
Deut 6:4-7
Matt 22:37-39

PROMISES
Psalms 76:11
Mark 5:33-37
I Kings 8:56
II Cor 1:20
Psalms 18:30
I Pet 1:24,25
James 1:21
II Pet 2:9

REMARRIAGE
I Cor 7:10,11
I Cor 7:15, 25-40
Matt 19:9
I Cor 7:39
I John 1:9
II Cor 6:14

REPENTANCE
Matt 4:17
Mark 1:14,15
Acts 17:30
Matt 11:20
Luke 15:7
Rom 2:4
Matt 9:13
Acts 3:19
Luke 13:3

RESEMTMENT
Eph 4:31
Gal 5:15-19
Heb 12:15
I John 2:9-11
I John 3:15
Rom 12:14-21
I John 1:9
Eph 4:32
Mark 11:25,26

4 of 6 Ministries of Forgiveness

EMOTIONAL TRIALS

Luke 17:24
I Pet 3:8,9

I Pet 1:6,9
Phil 4:8

I Pet 2:19
I Pet 4:12,13
I Pet 4:16;5:10

REST
Matt 11:28-30
Psalms 4:8
Heb 4:9
Psalms 94:12,13
Heb 4:3
Phil 4:6,7

SEX LIFE
Heb 13:4
I Cor 7:1-5
I Thes 4:3-5
I Cor 6:16-20

SUICIDE
Job 5:15
Psalms 34:1-7
John 10:10
Psalms 40
Psalms 42
Psalms 43
Psalms 51
Phil 4;6-8,19
Heb 7:25
Matt 7:7-11

SALVATION(Man's Need)
Is 64:6
Rom 3:10,23
Rom 5:12
Rom 6:23
Heb 9:27
I John 1:10
John 3:18

SEXUALITY IMMORALITY
Matt 5:27-30
Col 3:5-7
Matt 5:19,20
I Cor 6:9-20
Gal 5:16-18
Rom 6:15-23
Jude 6,7
I Thes 4:3-6

TEMPTATION
I Cor 10:12,13
Heb 2:18
James 1:2,3
James 1:12-14
I Pet 1:6
II Pet 2:19
Jude 24

SANCTIFICATION
II Cor 5:17
John 15:1-5
Phil 2:12,13
Eph 4:17-32
Eph 5:1-21
Col 3:1-17
Rom 8:1-14
I Tim 4:17
Rom 8:1-14
I Tim 4:17
II Pet 3:14
I Tim 4:17
Eph 6:10-17
James 4:7
Heb 12:1

SICKNESS
Psalms 41:3
Matt 4:23
John 11:4
James 5:15,16
III John 2
Is 53:4,5

TIMES OF TROUBLE
Psalms 50:15
Psalms 9:12
Psalms 91
John 16:33
Psalms 37:39,40
Psalms 121:5,8

SIN
Is 53:5-6
Is 59:1-2
John 8:34
Rom 3:23; 6:23
Gal 6:7,8
I John 1:9
James 4:17

TRAINING CHILDREN
Deut 6:6,7
Eoh 6:4
Col 3:21
I Tim 3:4
Prov 13:24
Heb 12:5-11
Psalms 127:3

SELF CENTEREDNESS
I Cor 13:5
James 3:14-16
Matt 20:26-28
Luke 9:23-25
I Cor 10:24
Rom 15:2,3

SORROW
Prov 10:22
Is 53:3
John 16:22
II Cor 6:10
Rev 214

STRENGTH
Psalms 27:14
Is 40:29-31
Is 41:10
Phil 4:19
Phil 4:13

TRUST
I Chron 29:11-12
Jer 32:17,26,27
Prov 3:5-6
Psalms 23
Psalms 27
Matt 3:23-27
Is 40:28-31
Is 43:1-3

SELF CONTROL
Gal 5:22,23
II Tim 1:17
II Pet 1:5,6
Titus 2:2-6
II Cor 10:4,5
I Thes 5:1-8

SUFFERING
Rom 8:18
II Cor 1:5
Phil 1:29
Phil 3:10
II Tim 2:12

UNPARDONABLE SIN
Matt 12:31,32
Mark 3:28-30
John 10:37,38
I Tim 1:12,13

SELF PITY
I Kings 19
Psalms 73
Prov 15:13

EMOTIONAL TRIALS

Luke 17:24
I Pet 3:8,9

REST
Matt 11:28-30
Psalms 4:8
Heb 4:9
Psalms 94:12,13
Heb 4:3
Phil 4:6,7

SALVATION(Man's Need)
Is 64:6
Rom 3:10,23
Rom 5:12
Rom 6:23
Heb 9:27
I John 1:10
John 3:18

SANCTIFICATION
II Cor 5:17
John 15:1-5
Phil 2:12,13
Eph 4:17-32
Eph 5:1-21
Col 3:1-17
Rom 8:1-14
I Tim 4:17
Rom 8:1-14
I Tim 4:17
II Pet 3:14
I Tim 4:17
Eph 6:10-17
James 4:7
Heb 12:1

SELF CENTEREDNESS
I Cor 13:5
James 3:14-16
Matt 20:26-28
Luke 9:23-25
I Cor 10:24
Rom 15:2,3

SELF CONTROL
Gal 5:22,23
II Tim 1:17
II Pet 1:5,6
Titus 2:2-6
II Cor 10:4,5
I Thes 5:1-8

SELF PITY
I Kings 19
Psalms 73
Prov 15:13

I Pet 1:6,9
Phil 4:8

SEX LIFE
Heb 13:4
I Cor 7:1-5
I Thes 4:3-5
I Cor 6:16-20

**SEXUALITY
IMMORALITY**
Matt 5:27-30
Col 3:5-7
Matt 5:19,20
I Cor 6:9-20
Gal 5:16-18
Rom 6:15-23
Jude 6,7
I Thes 4:3-6

SICKNESS
Psalms 41:3
Matt 4:23
John 11:4
James 5:15,16
III John 2
Is 53:4,5

SIN
Is 53:5-6
Is 59:1-2
John 8:34
Rom 3:23; 6:23
Gal 6:7,8
I John 1:9
James 4:17

SORROW
Prov 10:22
Is 53:3
John 16:22
II Cor 6:10
Rev 214

STRENGTH
Psalms 27:14
Is 40:29-31
Is 41:10
Phil 4:19
Phil 4:13

SUFFERING
Rom 8:18
II Cor 1:5
Phil 1:29
Phil 3:10
II Tim 2:12

I Pet 2:19
I Pet 4:12,13
I Pet 4:16;5:10

SUICIDE
Job 5:15
Psalms 34:1-7
John 10:10
Psalms 40
Psalms 42
Psalms 43
Psalms 51
Phil 4;6-8,19
Heb 7:25
Matt 7:7-11

TEMPTATION
I Cor 10:12,13
Heb 2:18
James 1:2,3
James 1:12-14
I Pet 1:6
II Pet 2:19
Jude 24

TIMES OF TROUBLE
Psalms 50:15
Psalms 9:12
Psalms 91
John 16:33
Psalms 37:39,40
Psalms 121:5,8

TRAINING CHILDREN
Deut 6:6,7
Eoh 6:4
Col 3:21
I Tim 3:4
Prov 13:24
Heb 12:5-11
Psalms 127:3

TRUST
I Chron 29:11-12
Jer 32:17,26,27
Prov 3:5-6
Psalms 23
Psalms 27
Matt 3:23-27
Is 40:28-31
Is 43:1-3

UNPARDONABLE SIN
Matt 12:31,32
Mark 3:28-30
John 10:37,38
I Tim 1:12,13

EMOTIONAL TRIALS

I John 1:9
I Cor 12:3

VENGENCE
Matt 5:38-40
Rom 12:17-21
Mark 18:21,22
Heb 10:30

VICTORY
II Chron 32:8
Rom 8:37
I Cor 15:57
II Cor 2:14
II Tim 2:19
I john 5:4
Rev 3:5
Rev 21:7

WEAK(For those who feel weak)
Psalms 142:3
Heb 3:19
Psalms 72:13
Eph 3:16
II Cor 12:9
Is 57:15

WITNESSING
Psalms 66:16
Mark 5:19
Luke 24:48
Acts 1:8

THE WORD GIVES THE PLAN OF SALVATION
Is 55:7
John 1:12
John 3:3
John 5:24
Rom 10:9,10
Eph 2:8,9
Titus 3:5
I John 1:9
Rev 3:20

WORRY
Matt 6:25-34
Phil 4:6,7
I Pet 5:6,7
Psalms 27:3,7
Joshua 1:9
Psalms 34:4
Psalms 116:6-8

TM

To Walk In Forgiveness You Must Walk In Forgiveness

Second part:

Un-Avoidable Bitterness

Email: iforgive@toforgive.org

Web: www.iforgivetoforgive.org

Un-Avoidable Bitterness

Un-Avoidable Bitterness: In the first part, I discussed about avoidable bitterness, or bitterness that can be avoided when practicing what the Word teaches. But now we need to discuss about the worst of bitterness, those things we cannot avoid by just following the word. Bad things happen to good people. Sometimes life just sends us a cruel twist.

Many children experience incest, which is sexual activity by family members to children too young to say "NO"! We hear almost daily of children some authorities are finding which have been sexually molested in ways too horrible to speak about. These children did not ask for nor give consent to such crimes.

Then there is rape, or sex forced on someone, usually to a woman, however, we are now learning about men who have been raped. Again, a sexual crime against someone not giving consent to the act. Nevertheless, it happens anyway!

There is also tragic events which happen to us which create an emotional challenge to our ability to function rationally. All these and other bad things occur, which cause bitterness in our lives. Moreover, this bitterness cannot be dealt with the same as with Avoidable Bitterness. However, the solution begins with the same basic scriptures of forgiveness. According to God's Word forgiveness still needs to happen for us to become set free of the bondage bitterness creates.

Psychology teaches that un-forgiveness (bitterness) creates an unwanted bondage between the one not forgiven and the one not forgiving!

In my seminar for the second session, I will have two metal chairs for all to see.

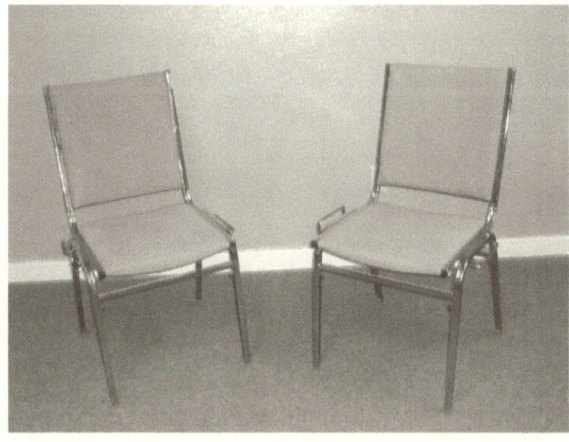

One chair, positioned on the right of the picture, will represent the person committing the sin and there will be a black box in the seat to represent the sin that person commits. I will ask for a woman to assist me in this demonstration. I will have the woman to sit in the chair to the audience's left. The chair representing the person who has committed the sin against her, will be to her left.

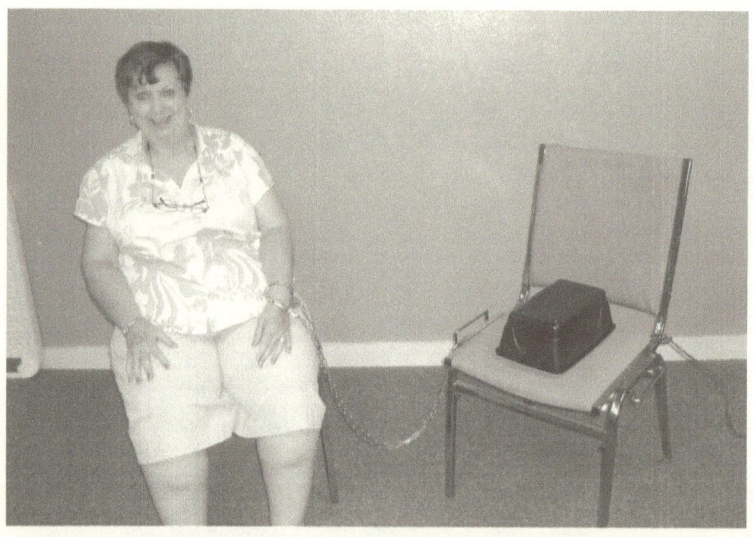

Now right off the bat, this is my wife and you cannot have her!

I began to talk about how bitterness creates a bondage of the one to which the sin has been committed upon, and that the other is the person who preformed the horrible act committed against her. She will, for the purpose of this demonstration, represent a woman who has been sexually assaulted sometime in her life. I have a chain with a pair of handcuffs attached to each end to the chair to her left. The chain is then wrapped around part of the chair on the sinners chair on the right so that both handcuffs are extended from that chair. I will then attach both handcuffs to the woman's left hand. The two handcuffs represent two types of bondage the demons lock us into with un-avoidable bitterness and sin. We will learn more as we continue.

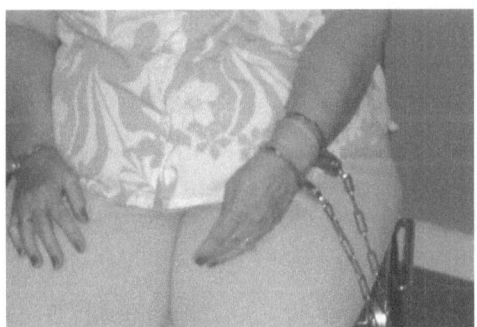

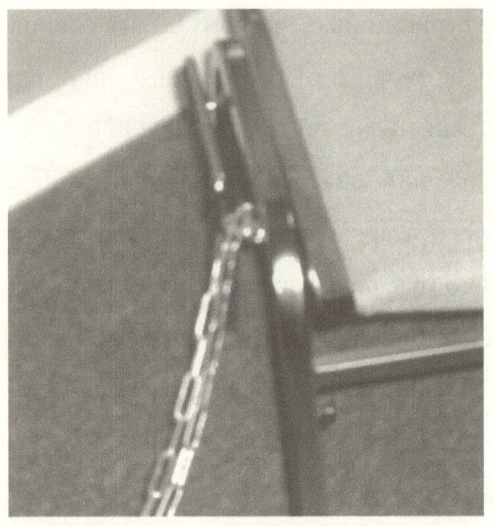

Note that the other person (chair) has **NO** handcuffs! Bondage is always on the victim.

We need to understand that mentally we are always conscious of the one who hurt us as we have allowed bitterness to dwell up inside us. This is part of what is called bondage. This bondage affects everything you wish to do. For one thing, that bondage affects our thinking. By this I mean that the act of sin committed against us is always on our mind!!! That despicable sin will be ever present in our daily thinking.

Let me ask you a question. When was the last time you pondered that event in your mind? How often have you plotted a plan to get even?

We daily devise ways to get even with the person with whom we are bitter. We cannot seem to conceive punishment horrible enough to satisfy the hurt inside us. Let me ask you another question and I want you to, from your heart, answer the question. Has it ever occurred to you that your daily plans of vindication simply have not worked? Do we not understand that bitterness or the bondage of bitterness affects our Moral Judgment? When bitterness sets in we begin to perceive every thing in our life from the screen of bitterness and with that self-justification.

The Bible teaches us that that bondage is a 'choice' we choose to make. We find in Romans 8:1 **"There is therefore now no condemnation on those who are in Christ Jesus..."** You see, it is our choice to harbor these ill feelings in our minds! We feel we have a right to find vindication or even more, to make the vindication ourselves! As a child of God, we have the right to think otherwise, we have the right to forgive! Remember, according to God, forgiveness is not an option.

Note that there is a Chair with a Box in the seat

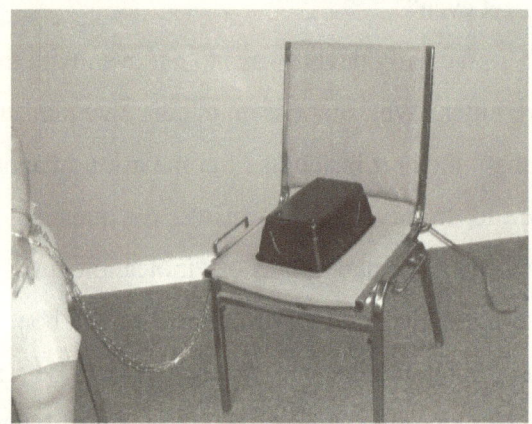

The black box represents the horrible act preformed against her. The Chair represents that person or individual which preformed the horrible act to her. She is handcuffed to the chair, or in reality, this shows that she is handcuffed to the person who committed the sin by the bonds of guilt and condemnation. She is now in bondage to that person. Note that she is the **<u>only one in handcuffs</u>**.

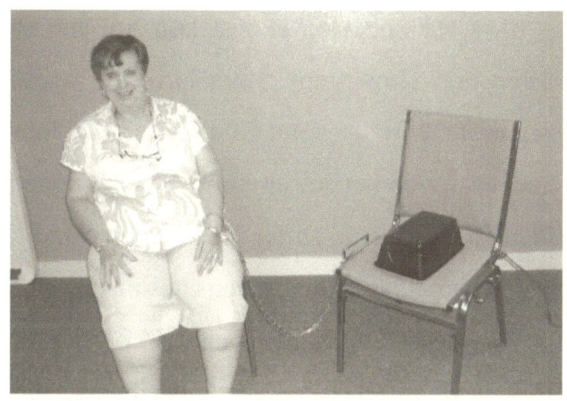

Not the individual, who committed the sin against her. Only she is in cuffs or in reality, the only one in bondage of bitterness. The bondage of the individual, who committed the sin, is in bondage to God but not in bondage to her! Also, note that she is in bondage to the individual and **not to his sin!**

We need to understand that we are **not** responsible for his *sin* before God. However, we **are** responsible for **our** attitude of *un-forgiveness* toward the individual before God. We are responsible for our own attitude and response to sin. We will not have to answer to God for the sin of the person hurting us. Nevertheless, we will have to answer to God for the way we dealt with that bitterness in our life.

The Nagging thought of the event and desired punishment to satisfy our hurt.

Ever wanting God to just lash out and strike him down with punishment! How many times have we wrestled in our mind the question of "Why does not God just "ZAP" him?" God is a God of justice but we do not see any justice being done in this situation. We feel God has left us to suffer the hurt alone and God does not seem to have done anything to the person causing our hurt.

Why don't we just help God "ZAP" him for what he has done to you! I have an electric cord plugged in to the wall and I have an electric cord attached to the chair. Let us say the electric cord from the wall is from God. Therefore, what we can do is to plug the two cords together! This way we can help God zap the person with whom you are in bondage with.

When I plug the two cords together, the electricity will go directly to that person and ZAP him good. This is what we want? Right? (Speaking to the woman).

What do you mean are you disturbed? We are simply trying to give God a little help in giving the person that hurt you what you feel they deserve. Why are you pulling at the handcuffs and chain? Oh, you say you will be "ZAPPED" also! Well, I guess that would be true. The electricity will go through the cord to the chair representing that man who has hurt you and continue through the chair to the chain and then to the handcuffs and then to you. Does this mean that if God wanted to "ZAP" the individual that you would get "ZAPPED" also? Well, that would be because, you are right. And that is the reason why God has not "ZAPPED" the person who has done this horrible act to you. Also, take note of the picture on next page that I have the two female plug ends, which cannot be plugged into each other; you were never in any real danger of electrical shock!

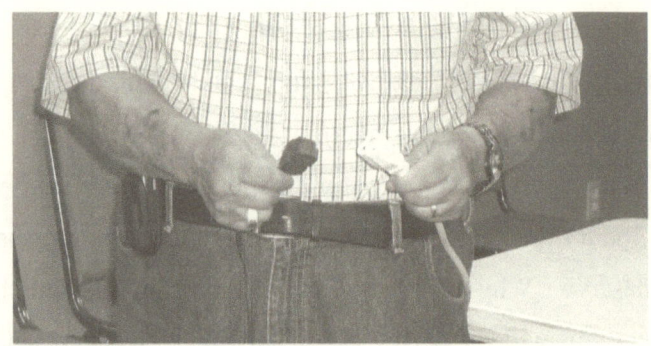

Let us look at Matt.13:24-30, verses commonly referred to as **"Wheat and the tare's parable".** Take a look again at vs. 28 & 29.

Matthew 13:28-29 (NKJV) *"[28] He said to them, 'An enemy has done this.' The servants said to him, 'Do you want us then to go and gather them up?' [29] But he said, 'No, lest while you gather up the tares you also uproot the wheat with them".*

The farmer did not want the wheat destroyed along with the tares. You see, 'tares' growing along side wheat looks the same as wheat. It is not until harvest time that the two can be told apart. As long as you remain in bondage to this individual, God cannot deal with his sin, as he would be in danger of destroying you. God may not deal with his sin until he dies and then God can deal with him justly, because by then the bondage you have with him will be broken and on the other side of death his sin can be dealt with justly. Do you wish to wait until his death to know his sin will be dealt with? It does not have to be until then for him to be punished. Only you can make that choice!

Has it ever occurred to you that it is **only you** disturbed about this thing? The person that committed the sin has not given the event another thought, while you think about it daily. How cunning the Devil is . . .

Not only has the devil attacked you physically with this event but also he now torments **you** with the thoughts of the event. You spend your daily life in torment while the one that committed the sin is seemingly going on with their life! The Devil has put a double whammy on you! **The Word teaches that in order to be set free of this we must forgive!**

This is not an easy thing to do! Right? Then the Devil torments us more by now inserting another lie to help you stay in bitterness! He cunningly inserts a common lie, but presenting it as Biblical and that is to forgive the person you ***must forgive what they have done***! I do not know about you but I find that that is just about impossible for me! In addition, I would surmise that you will come to the same conclusion. Right?

Listen to this truth ... Let me ask you a question. Does God forgive sin? Give thought to this question before you answer! If you answer yes, then you truly do not understand the justice of God. God has NEVER, ever, forgiven sin; rather He judged sin on the cross! If God does not forgive sin, then **God** will not ask you to forgive any sin that was done to you! Do you understand what I just said? God does not ask you to forgive that sin that was done to you! Listen to me…**EVEN GOD DOES NOT FORGIVE SIN!** God has, does, and always will hate sin! However, He has never forgiven any sin. Stay with me now! The Word commands us to "Be angry and sin not" How does he do this. He **FORGIVES THE SINNER** (Person) but never forgives the **SIN!** Paul writes in **Eph 1:7** *"In Him we have redemption through His blood, the forgiveness of sins, according to the riches of His grace.* Note the word <u>we</u> (as a person) have redemption with the forgiveness of our sin. Note John in **I John 2:12** *"I write to you, little children, because your sins are forgiven <u>you</u> for His name's sake."* God always has and always will hate SIN! He hated sin so much that he judged Sin on the Cross! But he loves you so much that He will forgive you of your sin.

FORGIVENESS – THE CARNAL WAY

The world teaches that you must forgive what the person did! You see that to do this, means that we are to "excuse", justify the sin, or better yet let them off the hook! If we do this, we no longer would hold that sin to their charge! Do I want their sin excused? I do not think so! That sin must receive justice for me to find peace. Yet, this is exactly what is happening in our court system today. The courts are slapping the hands of the sinner and excusing what they have done.

FORGIVENESS – THE GRACE WAY!

God's Word teaches that we must forgive the <u>person</u> for what they did. Note I said the person not the sin. You cannot excuse, justify, or forgive sin. You must release the judgment of that sin to God, and then **we** will no longer be holding that sin to their charge in our mind. Now just how do we do this you may ask?

SEPARATE THE PERSON FROM THE SIN!

We must learn to forgive the way God forgave us! I must learn to forgive and treat the sin and person the way God dealt with our sin and us. He separated us from our sin. By this, I mean He chose to view my sin separate from me. If I hate the <u>person</u> **and** the <u>sin,</u> I am at enmity with God! You see, while I hate the person, I hate the person God loves! I have declared my judgment greater that God's judgment of Justice. I have taken on a right God has never given to me, that is to sit in judgment over someone.   However, it I hate the sin and forgive the person, I am in agreement with the God of Love!

View the shadow / clear figurine!

I love this devise. This box is made at right angles with one side made of smoked plastic transparent glass while the other side is made of clear transparent plastic glass. In the center between the two sheets of plastic is a figurine, which represents man. Notice his uniform. He is a fireman, waiting to put out the fire of bitterness.

The dark side represents the sin or the carnal side of the person in the center. As we look through the smoked glass, which represents his carnal nature or sin or from the carnal perspective. Note that I am looking at this individual through his sin. I will always see his sin _**first**_! When I view others through their sin, I get a distorted view of them. No matter how I view them through the smoked glass, I cannot keep from seeing them wrapped or enveloped in their sin. I am unable to separate him from his sin. The sad thing is that we tend to believe that God looks at us the same way. We believe He always sees our sin first and will deal with us through sin. I will begin to hate God for allowing this sin on me. I will become double minded. I will try to love and hate at the same time, all the while trying to convince myself that I love God while hating my brother.

Now look through the clear side (which is Grace {love} Perspective) and we find that we are looking at him while viewing his sin behind him, not the individual through his sin! I can now get a much clearer concept of the individual as I am looking at the individual and seeing him/her as they are, as opposed to viewing him/her through their sin. I can now understand that his sin is not the same as the individual. I also can now understand that this is the way God views me. I can now understand how God can look at me in love and separates my sin from me. God has always demonstrated His love toward us as an individual while viewing my sin as sin. Many of us love God with one mind while hating the person with another part of our mind. I am a *"Cartoon Christian"*! I prevent God from dealing with the person and their sin because I refuse to separate the individual from their sin. I am asking God to judge with double jeopardy!

Note figure 4. **Using the Criminal / Civil diagram on the next page:**

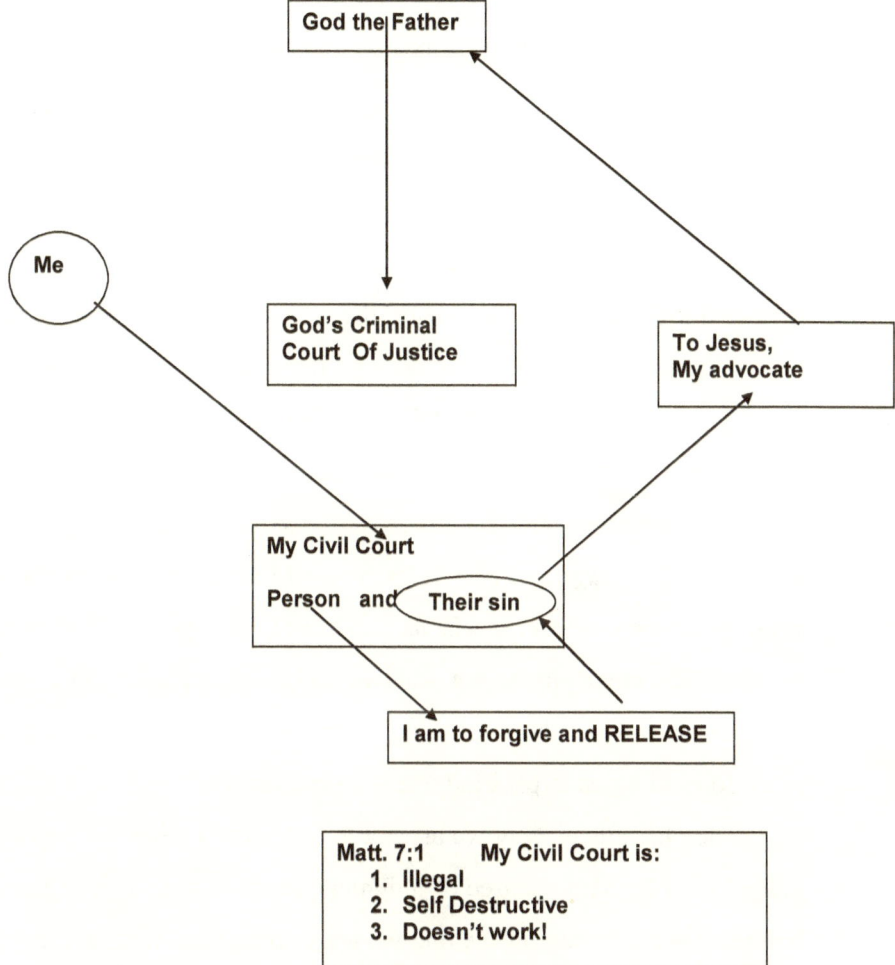

Figure 4 Our civil (self) court compared to God's court of Justice.

There area three main reasons why our civil court system will not work. They are listed below.

a.   Civil (self) court is illegal Matt 7:1

b.   Civil (self) court is self destructive

c.   Civil (self) court just simply **doesn't work!**

We play a little game in our mind. We will place the individual in our personal civil court and will then try, judge, and execute that person <u>daily</u>. We will, in our mind, execute that individual in a thousand different ways. However, the problem is that tomorrow they are in our civil court again and we find them just as guilty as the day before. We need to understand that judging the individual in our little civil court is according to the Word of God - illegal!

Read Matthew 7:1, 2 *"Judge not, that you be not judged.* (2) *For with what judgment you judge, you will be judged, and with the same measure you use, it will be measured back to you."* Here we see that God clearly does not want us to be judging each other even though it seems like the right thing to do. A direct command is given to us, forbidding us to pass judgment on each other.

Then he tells us why we are not to judge each other. We will be judged with the same degree of judgment we gave out. The degree of bitterness we are judging the one we are in bitterness with will be the degree of bitterness we will be judged back with in life. Your judgment will come back on **YOU**! Bitterness always lowers the moral standard of the person looking in bitterness, and not only that, bitterness will create in you the same character of the one bitter against.

Lastly, we need to understand is that our civil court of bitter judgment just simply does not work! You would think we would catch on to this fact when we keep bringing that person up in our civil court again and again and again, day after day after day, . . . well you get the picture.

God gives us the plan of forgiveness for those who hurt us. God teaches us that he forgave us for His sake first! In doing this, he did not forgive me of my sins, but rather He has forgiven me for his sake. He now does not choose to carry any bitterness due to the sin I committed toward his Son. This keeps Him clear to forgive me of my sin should I choose to ask for forgiveness. Because God has already forgiven me for His own sake, I can now know that He does not look at me in judgment but rather looks at me with mercy. I know that at any time I can come to him with repentance, knowing His actions will be in love and not condemnation. I know that I will be forgiven! He was teaching me that I had to be ready and able to forgive that person when they repented. For God to do this He had to be able to separate me from my sin . . . and to do that he needed to forgive me for His sake first. Now when He looks at my sin He sees past me and can look at my sin and hate that sin with justice. This way He kept his heart focused on me not my sin. Keep in mind that it was Satan guiding me in my sin, not myself. God could now focus on me and not my sin. He could keep His heart ready to forgive me when I chose to repent. Forgiving me for His sake did **not excuse me from my sin**! It just proves God is in alignment with His Justice and Grace. I now must learn to do the same to the person or individual who harmed me. I must separate that person from the event done to me! I need to remember that it was Satan working through the person who hurt me, just as the enemy is trying to work through me to create bondage. I do not deserve to be in bondage. You understand, Satan knows that because I do not fully understand who I am in Christ, all he has to do is to point and accuse and I will take up the hurt. It is not right for me to hurt and that person who sinned against me not to hurt. Nevertheless, to correct this I need to learn to forgive that individual for **my** sake so that the enemy cannot push me into bondage through bitterness. Forgiving that person does not excuse the sin committed toward me, rather it opens the door for God to deal (zap) them in judgment. It is not the question of whether that individual deserves to be forgiven, but rather it is the question of do 'I' deserve to be forgiven and set free. I need to choose or accept the truth that that person is not worth me being in bitterness!

I now move the black box off the chair and set it on the floor.

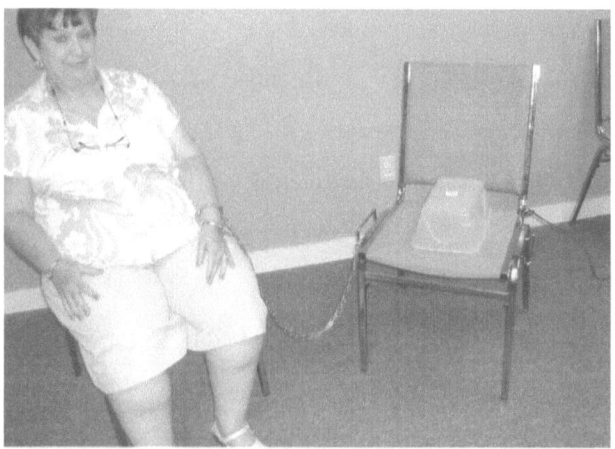

As I lift the black box off the chair there is now a white box on chair, representing his soul or life, not his sin. I have released his sin unto Jesus, my advocate. Jesus then submits that sin to his Father, the only true judge.

Take note of the words of Paul in Col. 3:13 *"If any man has a quarrel against any; even as Christ forgave you, so also must you."* God's plan for us in these situations goes totally against the carnal reasoning. **God's plan for this forgiveness is two fold.** God first forgives me for **HIS** sake. He did this so He could come to me in a spirit of forgiveness. He knew I needed to perceive Him as Just and Righteous in order for me to accept His forgiveness.   He could then say that He indeed LOVED ME! He loved me while I still was in my sin and condemned to Hell!   Bear in mind that I had yet to have repented when he declared he loved me. While God had forgiven me, it was for his sake not MINE! Because he forgave me while still a sinner, <u>He could not be charged with hating me,</u> He does in fact still hate my sin. God has ***never*** forgiven my SIN!!! He redeemed my sin cursed spirit, and cut away my dead spirit and cast is as far as the East is from the West,   (learn more in my book 'GRACE OF JUSTICE') and took my sin covered soul and washed it in the blood of Jesus to make my soul as white and pure as show.

He STILL hates my sin but forever loves me! I must now learn to do the same toward that individual who hurt me! I need to understand that forgiving for my sake does not produce **RECONCILATION** nor does it in any way produce **RESTORTATION** between them and me!!! I need to, for my sake, forgive the person while still hating the sin he or she committed. You can use the following prayer as a guide for your prayer of forgiveness.

Pray the following prayer of "Forgiving Another"

PRAYER FOR FORGIVING ANOTHER

Forgiveness is a choice, a decision of your will. Forgiveness is not an option. Since God requires you to forgive, it is something you CAN do! By forgiving, you let the other person off YOUR hook, but they are NOT off God's hook. Ask God to bring to your mind the people you need to forgive by praying the following prayer aloud:

Dear Heavenly Father,
I thank You for the riches of your kindness, forbearance and patience toward me, knowing that Your kindness has led me to repentance (Romans 2:4). I confess that I have not shown that same kindness and patience toward those who have hurt me. Instead, I have held on to my anger, bitterness and resentment toward them. Bring to my mind all the people I need to forgive in order that I may do so now, In Jesus' name, Amen.

For every painful memory, you have for each person pray this prayer aloud:

Lord,
I choose to forgive (Name the Person) for (Say what they did that hurt you)even though it made me feel bitter. *Share the painful*

feelings.   I forgive <u>(Name)</u> unconditionally for these things that brought hurt into my life.

I drop every charge I have brought against <u>(Name)</u> and give up the right to ever charge him/her again for this offense.

I cancel every judgment I have made against <u>(Name)</u> regarding this offense.

In the name of my Lord, Jesus Christ, I release <u>(Name)</u> from all responsibility to me for the hurt which (<u>his / her</u>) behavior provoked in me. Instead, I assume all responsibility for having chosen to hold onto this offense.

Heavenly Father, I drop every charge I have had against you for permitting this to happen to me. Forgive me for any way I have blamed you in this offense.

I forgive <u>myself</u> for every wrong attitude, action, and reaction associated with this offense.

Heavenly Father, as I have now forgiven (Name) for the hurt I have experienced, forgive me for my hurt, bitterness, anger and forgiveness.

Holy Spirit, come and heal my thoughts, my emotions and my memories from all the damage and defilement caused by this offense, Thank you, Father, for my healing.

I declare and request these things in the authority of my Lord and Savior, Jesus Christ. Amen

NAME_____DATE_____

****
****

I NOW REMOVE "ONE" HANDCUFF

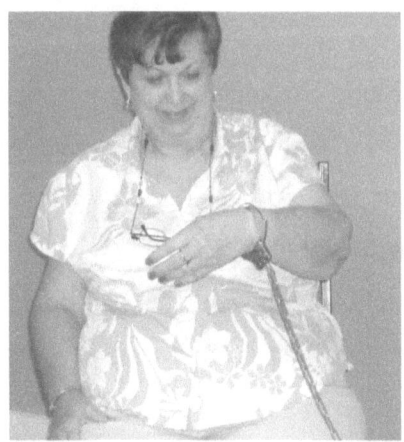

Are you **STILL HANDCUFFED? I ask. Then there must be another problem, and it could be that there is more bitterness due to sexual offence in your life**. Very seldom are we bound by just one problem. Quite often resolving the one bitterness reveals a second problem in our life that has been masked by the first bitterness.

As bitterness 'bonds' us to the individual, so does sex out of marriage! In **I Cor. 6:16** *"Or do you not know that he who is joined to a harlot is ONE BODY with her?" For "the two," He says, "shall become one flesh."* Which causes us to ask a new question of just what constitutes marriage in the Bible? What does the phrase "Two shall become one flesh!" mean? It means that each time we have sex with another person we have preformed the marriage act which crates a Soul Bond!!!

Now do not be looking around but some here may actually be married to another person because of sinful sex! The Devil knows this and places another curse upon the individual forced into sexual behavior. This needs to be **RENOUNCED** or if you please, spiritually **DIVORCED** as the sinful act of sin of the Soul Bond. You still need to pray another prayer. Consider the following as a guide.

PRAYER REGARDING ANY EXTRAMARITAL SEXUAL ENCOUNTER WITH ANOTHER:

Dear Father, I confess the unwholesomeness and wrongness of the relationship between _____ (Name the person involved with.) and myself. I confess that I had sex with ___ Name specifically the activities you were involved in) ___ Thank you for your forgiveness. I renounce the behavior I have confessed and ask you to break that bond. I declare and decree, in the name of Jesus, a complete and final severance between us. And in Jesus' name, I command all fragments of my soul that I lost during my encounter with ___ (name) ___ soul to be returned to ___ him / her ___. Holy Spirit, come and completely re-unite and heal my total personality from the injuries done to me in this relationship. I receive that work by faith as a work of God's grace.

NAME_____

DATE_____

Following are other sexual sins of which one might be guilty of and have a need to pray a prayer to break that bondage.

PRAYER REGARDING BEING SEXUALLY MOLESTED AS A CHILD

I renounce the lie that I need to give my body to someone so that I can be accepted and special. I announce the truth that I am accepted by Christ just as I am. I also renounce the lie that I am evil or dirty as a result of my molestation.

Thank you, Lord that you know that I was only a child who needed love and acceptance. I receive your forgiveness for any way that I might have cooperated, and I choose to forgive myself and recognize that I am indeed forgiven.

Thank you, Jesus.

Name:_____**Date**_____/_____
_/_____

PRAYER TO USE IF YOU HAVE BEEN RAPED:

I renounce any bondage brought into my life by a sexual encounter that I did not ask for and did not consent to, when I was raped. I also renounce the lie that I am evil or dirty as a result of this rape. I renounce the lie that I am unwanted and unlovable. I renounce the lie that I deserved what I got. I declare and decree, in the name of Jesus, a complete and final severance of this bondage between __(Name of 'the rapist")__ and myself. And in Jesus' name, I command all fragments of my soul that I lost during this assault by __(Name of 'the rapist')__ to be returned to me. I release all residue from __(name's of 'the rapist's)__ soul to be returned to __him/her__. Holy Spirit, come and completely re-unite and heal my total personality from the injuries done to me by this assault. I now declare that I am now free to love and to be loved in a healthy relationship. I receive that design by faith as a work of God's Grace.

In the Name of Jesus I pray…

Name:_____

Date:_____/_____/_____

I WOULD NOW REMOVE SECOND HANDCUFF!

 Many of us are carrying around bondage of our past sins of youth or an evil act of sexual sin committed on us, but needs, nevertheless, to be confessed and forgiven.

Been there, done that!

And yet, I continue to come across people who have been to the alter, on their knees and have confessed their prior sin and a few months later are fighting with the same guilt again. Well, I spent no little time in prayer and Bible study to learn the "why" of this dilemma. To come to the answer we need to confirm some things in our life.

One of the first things we need to confirm is our new birth experience with Jesus Christ as our LORD and Savior. Many were never taught that receiving Christ and becoming saved meant making Jesus the LORD of our life also. Look at Matthew 16: 14-18. Peter is asked who he thinks Jesus is and Peter confesses that Jesus is "the Christ". Being a Jew Peter knew that the term "the Christ" meant "the Messiah or the anointed one of the Lord" and was confessing that Jesus was now his LORD, or the Lordship of the Christ. Jesus in verse 18 states that upon that confession of Lordship, Jesus would build his church. If this was never the intent of your confession, then you need to re-confirm the intent of your heart of that confession of asking for forgivingness by now verbally submitting to the Lordship of Jesus Christ in our heart!

If we have confirmed that we have indeed received Jesus as personal Lord and Savior, then we need to confirm in our heart that when we prayed a prayer of forgiving the individual and releasing their sin to Jesus, that we indeed meant it. You see, once we have prayed a prayer forgiving that person, we need to understand that they were forgiven in heaven also. No, we did not forgive their sin for them in heaven, we simply forgave them personally for our sakes, and that was recorded in heaven for all eternity. However, if we are again experiencing the feelings of guilt or condemnation, this begs the question, "Did the individual commit the sin again?" If our answer is a "NO" then we need to understand that we cannot re-forgive that individual again!!!

This must mean there is another problem then!!!

We need to understand that the devil understands all of the principals of the Word and because we do not know and understand who we are, the enemy will beat us to death with the principals of truth against us. Let's look at Matthew 5:28 which states that if I look upon a woman and lust after her, I have committed the actual sin of physical sex As I begin to rethink again about the sin committed against me, I begin to play it out in my mind and I in fact, become guilty of **that very sin!** I am now committing that sin *MYSELF!*

Consider John in 1 John 3:15 *"If I look upon a brother in hate, I have committed murder"* You see that If I begin hating that person *again* by beginning to think about it again, I am now committing *MURDER!* The truth is that I now need to repent to God for both sins! You understand that in the Word I am commanded never to think on this sin again.

Paul writes in Phil 4:8 **"What so ever things…"** I am to be thinking on things which are good rather than on the things which are bad in my life. Many will try to tell me that they have to think these bad thoughts. Let me set that straight!

SATAN CANNOT MAKE YOU THINK ON THESE THINGS!

Read again John 1:12 (KJV) *"[12] But as many as received him, to them gave he power to become the sons of God, even to them that believe on his name:"*

John reminds us that we have power from God to believe or think or not believe or think as we choose. The following is a prayer for having entertained *__again__* the thoughts of the actions of the person who sinned against you. You have already prayed the prayer of forgiveness and know that you once forgave that person. However, you have allowed the enemy to activate the memory of that done against you and now you have begun to entertain the old "Personal Civil Court" against the person.

YOU ARE NOW THE ONE COMMITING **THAT SIN**! Now you are the one guilty for that sin and you must ask God for your forgiveness of entertaining those thoughts. You now need to pray the prayer of forgiveness, on the next page, for harboring those thoughts.

Prayer of forgiveness for entertaining thoughts of the enemy.

Dear Heavenly Father,

I have sinned in that I allowed the enemy to inject the thoughts of the sin (Name of Person I have already forgiven) had done to me, but that I had already forgiven, but I have again entertained them in my mind. I realize that in doing so I am now guilty of the sin (Name of Person who committed this sin to me) had committed to me. I am now guilty of the same sin of (name the offense committed to you) as well as the sin of murder as I entertained the thoughts of hatred and murder in my own mind. I now repent (turn away from) from entertaining the thoughts that the enemy injected in my mind and I claim your forgiveness of the sins I am now committing in thought and I also choose to forgive myself in repentance and declare that from hence forth I will only think on things that are of good report and are uplifting. Thank you for forgiving me and I choose now never to entertain those thoughts the enemy seeks to pun in my mind again. In Jesus' name, I pray.

Signed:_____Date:

_____

Pray the prayer about that "thought" sin you have committed and then date and sign.

Make a commitment not to allow that thought to remain in your mind. The devil is a liar; you are a Saint, redeemed by the blood of the Lamb and as such, you also have the mind of Christ. As a Saint you have been given all the tools to accomplish all that Jesus ask of you. You have been given:

1. The blood of Jesus
2. The Grace of God
3. The indwelling power of the Holy Spirit
4. The Word

All the tools you need to defeat the enemy in your life. Because of this, you have the right to refuse to entertain those thoughts again. Give it to Jesus immediately. If you will follow this, you will never again be haunted by the guilt or condemnation again. However, I will instead, learn to live in the peace and Grace of Jesus Christ. Allow me to share a principle for you to enact to stop the evil thoughts Satan injects into your mind. Begin counting to 100 in your thought mind. When you get to 20, begin reading or quoting a passage of scripture aloud. Now what happened to the thought process of counting? When Satan wants you to think on evil things, you begin to speak verbally good things, any thing good, but the Word of God would be better!

Apply these principals and you will find inner healing for your bitterness and hurts. We cannot get away from people trying to hurt us and to create bitterness in our life. However, we don't have to ACCEPT there hurts nor the bitterness hurled at us. We are to walk in the Grace of Christ and rise above these levels of condemnation. We need to remember who we are in Christ Jesus and that we are to allow the Grace of God to overcome all sin within us.

Forgiveness is yours! Only you have to grasp it in your heart and mind.

Remember **2 Peter 1:10 (KJV)** *"[10] Wherefore the rather, brethren, give diligence to make your* **calling** *and* **election** *sure: for if ye do these things, ye shall never fall: "*

Marvin L, Ward was born in Denver City, Texas on April 12, 1941. He moved around as a boy until moving to Rotan, Texas. There in a small Baptist church he asks Jesus to come into his life at the ripe age of 12.

He joined the USAF in October 1960 and traveled all the way to Oklahoma! There in Oklahoma he met the one and only, Wilma Wilson, to become is life long companion. They were married on June 8, 1967. He was called to pastor his first church in October 1967, to the Oak Street Baptist Church in Kingfisher, Oklahoma.

He has pastored for 18 years in Texas and Oklahoma. In 1984 he became Spirit filled and moved to the Dallas area and began attending the Church on the Rock Rockwall, Rockwall, Texas. Continuing to grow and learn how to walk in the Spirit, he later joined the North Church, in Carrollton, Texas. There he became a Faith Based Board Certified Pastoral Therapists and began counseling.

The Lord began to lead him to formulate a seminar on bitterness and forgiveness based on his life experiences and studies. Moreover, from this experience he began, on the encouragement of friends and especially his wife, Wilma, to put the material into books. You can go to his Web page and read more of his ministry as well as purchase one of his books:

www.iforgivetoforgive.org